‘A blunt and confronting perspective on foreign affairs. An important read for all Australians and an essential read for Australian politicians.’

Rex Patrick, Australian Senator (2019–2022) and former submariner, Royal Australian Navy

‘It is a rare international relations book that provides readers with a Eureka moment, the moment when the oddities of the thread of logic that underpins a nation’s security and foreign policy practices suddenly makes sense. *Subimperial Power* is that kind of book, one that will find a well-deserved place on university reading lists and hopefully make its way into the hands of Australia’s policy makers and security thinkers.

Fernandes is a fluid and accomplished writer, yet many readers will still find this book difficult to read. This is because Fernandes challenges long-held yet fallacious beliefs and, in doing so, he strips the edifice of Australian security and foreign policy to its core and exposes truths that will make some uncomfortable. *Subimperial Power* is a short but disruptive work that should be read and talked about, and Fernandes’ analysis deserves to become the foundation of the next Foreign Affairs and Defence White Papers. I give it my full endorsement.’

Albert Palazzo, former Director of War Studies, Australian Army Research Centre

A blunt and compelling perspective [illegible]. An important read for all Australians and an essential read for Australian politicians.

[illegible] Adrian [illegible]
and [illegible]

[illegible] relations [illegible] with a [illegible], the [illegible] policy [illegible] that [illegible] important [illegible] hands of Australian policy makers and [illegible].

[illegible] a fluid and [illegible] readers will still find this book difficult [illegible] because [illegible] work that should be read and talked about, and [illegible] analysis [illegible] Foreign Affairs and Defence [illegible] underscored.

[illegible] former Director [illegible]
[illegible]

SUB-IMPERIAL POWER

Australia in the International Arena

CLINTON FERNANDES

MELBOURNE UNIVERSITY PRESS
An imprint of Melbourne University Publishing Limited
Level 1, 715 Swanston Street, Carlton, Victoria 3053, Australia
mup-contact@unimelb.edu.au
www.mup.com.au

First published 2022

Reprinted 2023

Cover design by Philip Campbell Design
Typeset by Sonya Murphy, Adala Studio
Printed in Australia by McPherson's Printing Group

A catalogue record for this book is available from the National Library of Australia

9780522879261 (paperback)
9780522879278 (ebook)

Contents

Acknowledgements

I AM GRATEFUL TO UNSW Canberra for an atmosphere conducive to research: the Academy Library at UNSW Canberra, especially Deborah Despard and Rohana Liyanage in the Acquisitions Team and Michael Lemmer and Anna Papoulis in the Liaison Team; Hans Riesen, Michael Frater and UNSW Canberra's Research Infrastructure Scheme for providing access to the Bloomberg Professional Terminal; the Future Operations Research Group at UNSW Canberra, especially David Kilcullen; UNSW Canberra Space, especially Andrew Lambert; UNSW Institute for Cyber Security; and the Naval Studies Group and the Maritime Security Research Group at UNSW Canberra.

This book emerged from engaging with the ideas of a number of people and groups. I thank them, noting of course that they are not responsible for the final product: Rodrigo Acuna, Fiona Allen, Dorothea Anthony, Georgina Arnott, David Austin, Mark Beeson, Claudianna Blanco, Robert Boughton, Alison Broinowski, David Brophy, Scott Burchill,

Robert Buzzanco, Noam Chomsky, Susan Connelly, Cameron Coventry, Peter Cronau, Peter Curtis, Peter Dennis, David Dixon, Klaus Dodds, Philip Dorling, Deborah Durnan, Juan Federer, James Fitzgerald, Lewis Frederickson, James Goldrick, Jacob Grech, Andrew Greene, Steven Jones, Bernard Keane, David Kilcullen, Natalie Klein, Peter Kornbluh, Michael Leach, Pablo Leighton, David Lee, David Lovell, Michael McKinley, Joe McLaren, Robert McLaughlin, Humphrey McQueen, Florencia Melgar, Shaun Nelson, Albert Palazzo, Scott Parkin, Rex Patrick, Mark Pavlick, Robert Redwine, John Reeve, David Richardson, Marcus Salvagno, Vince Scappatura, Andrew Serdy, Jay Spain-Taylor, Sean Starrs, Craig Stockings, Cait Storr, Geoffrey Taylor, Brian Toohey, Caroline Yarnell and Jian Zhang; Jeff Robinson and Jane Hardy at the Department of Foreign Affairs and Trade; Andrew Gilbert and Lewis Frederickson of the Air Power Development Centre and former Chief of Air Force Fellows at UNSW Canberra; the Under Investigation team at the Nine Network: Liz Hayes, Eleanor Sprawson and Alex Chance; and my fellow panelists John Lee, David Brophy, Jason Yat-Sen Li, Malcolm Davis, Annette Lu, Grant Newsham, David Kilcullen and Jim Fanell; the *Q+A* team at the ABC: Hamish Macdonald and my fellow panellists: Jacinta Carroll, Annika Smethurst, Dennis Richardson and Nick Xenophon; Natalie Lowrey, Mara Bonacci, Lee Tan, Jemma Bailey, May Kotsakis, Claire Burgess, Barry Lalley, Jemma Bailey and James Goodman of Aid/Watch.

This book began its existence at *Arena*, a quarterly publication produced by the Arena Collective. I thank Alison Caddick and Sarah Bailey for their help. Aspects of it were presented at an Arena conjuncture meeting. I thank the participants: Alison Caddick, John Hinkson, Richard King, Guy Rundle, Melinda Hinkson, Paul James, Carlos Morreo and Timothy Ström.

I thank my lawyer, Ian Latham, and my solicitor, Hugh Macken, for staying the course for years, pro bono.

I thank Margaret Douglas for her support.

I thank Nathan Hollier and the team from Melbourne University Publishing, and Cathryn Game for her editorial expertise.

Derek Fernandes helped throughout with his shrewd judgement of geopolitics combined with a deep sympathy for its victims. Deb Salvagno provided a dynamic sounding-board for many of the ideas in this book.

I dedicate this book to the memory of the late Dr Andrew McNaughtan.

Introduction

HOW DOES AUSTRALIAN FOREIGN policy work, and for whom?

One answer is that it serves the national interest. Australia's first White Paper on foreign and trade policy was called *In the National Interest*. Published in 1997, it said the national interest involved 'the hard-headed pursuit of the interests which lie at the core of foreign and trade policy: the security of the Australian nation and the jobs and standard of living of the Australian people. In all that it does in the field of foreign and trade policy, the Government will apply this basic test of the national interest.'[1]

Another answer is that Australia is a middle power and behaves as a good international citizen.[2] In this reading, usually associated with the Australian Labor Party, '[G]ood international citizenship is a critical driver to achieving a secure and prosperous Australia.' It means 'the pursuit of enlightened self-interest' because 'enhancing the rules-based international order' and 'promoting respect for universal human rights' is the way to achieve 'long-term peace and prosperity for the

Australian people'. This means rock-solid support for the alliance with the United States, support for regional engagement, and support for the United Nations and other multilateral institutions to solve global challenges. Labor might 'differ over emphasis and approach' with the Coalition but, as Labor's foreign affairs spokesperson said, 'We are fortunate to have broad agreement on the component parts.'[3]

There is broad agreement, to be sure. A leading Liberal politician assured his audience that the Labor Party had no monopoly on supporting the US alliance: it was a Liberal government that negotiated the 1951 ANZUS Treaty, which 'remains the central pillar in our national security framework'. Likewise regional engagement: the first external affairs minister to go on a wide-ranging tour of Asia did so in 1934 and came from the conservative side of politics. There was a difference of emphasis: the Liberal tradition, he said, involved 'a pragmatic rather than a dewy-eyed view' of the United Nations and other multilateral institutions. A 'common sense approach' to such institutions and to foreign policy more generally 'has been the hallmark of successive Liberal governments'.[4]

In more recent years, a new explanation has emerged: Australian foreign policy defends a 'rules-based international order'. This concept was central to the Defence White Paper of 2016, the Foreign Policy White Paper of 2017 and numerous other speeches and policy documents. One of the authors of the 2017 White Paper explained that Australia will be 'more secure and more prosperous in a global order based on agreed rules rather than one based on the exercise of power alone'. He said there are times when 'Australia has to take responsibility for its own security and prosperity' because the rules and institutions are not adequate. This is old wine in new bottles. After all, '[T]his is not an entirely new proposition for Australia. We have never, for example, relied solely on the rules-based order for our security.'[5]

This book examines the claim that Australia is a middle power trying to uphold a rules-based international order. Rejecting these euphemisms, it shows that Australia is a subimperial power upholding a US-led imperial order. Chapter 1, 'A subimperial power', explains that an empire is 'a relationship, formal or informal, in which one state controls the effective political sovereignty of others'.[6] Being an imperial power means exerting a controlling influence on other countries' sovereignty. Control can be achieved without conquering colonies or directly ruling foreign lands. It can be established through economic, social or cultural dependence, political collaboration between both countries' elites, the threat or use of military force, *coups d'état*, intelligence operations, trade agreements and investment treaties. Today the United States sits at the apex of a hierarchically structured imperial system.

Australia is not an exploited neocolony in the US-led imperial system but a subimperial power. As such, it is an active, eager participant in the US-led order. Like that other subimperial power, Israel, Australia has a capable, technologically advanced military and a number of intelligence agencies that operate in the region and far afield to uphold the US-led order. Australia's trade and investment agreements are organised with a similar goal in mind. Public opinion is strongly in favour of the alliance with the United States. Australia has a stable government, strong economic performance and educated citizens. It is not located in a strategically crucial area of the world, unlike Israel, but compensates for its less vital strategic location by its actions: frequent military deployments, clandestine espionage operations to support the United States, hosting intelligence facilities, foreign policy mimicry and so on.

Chapter 2, 'The rules-based international order', explores how the system works and Australia's role in it. A rules-based international order is not an inclusive order created for the benefit of humanity. It does not mean a peaceful and harmonious system, despite its benign-sounding name. International orders are power politics by procedural means. They entrench the power of powerful states and help them exclude and subdue their rivals. The major international orders of the past four centuries were 'orders of exclusion', designed by dominant powers to ostracise and outcompete rivals. In 1648, the Peace of Westphalia, which ended the Thirty Years' War, was designed to undermine the authority of the Catholic Church and the Holy Roman Empire. It conferred autonomy on the hundreds of smaller principalities on which the empire was built—known today as 'state sovereignty'—and made the empire harmless by shattering its unity and cohesion. In 1815, the post-Napoleonic peace established in the Concert of Europe was designed so that conservative monarchies could counter the rise of liberal revolutionary regimes. The third international order involved 'the primacy of the first hegemonic actor in history to be a full liberal democracy, the United States of America'.[7]

After World War II, the North Atlantic Treaty Organization (NATO) defended a European order that kept the Soviet Union out, Germany down and the United States in—in charge, that is. This is hardly surprising: as Lance Reddick argued while the war was still raging in 1943, peace planning occurred within an environment of competition between British and American capitalism.[8] The post–World War II order was built on suppressing the anti-fascist resistance in Europe and reconstructing the old order by bringing back the fascist collaborators. That was a major objective of US and British forces as they landed on the continent in 1944.[9] It helped create the United Nations in order to entrench postwar US world leadership; the United Nations would amplify rather than constrain US power abroad and help manage American public opinion of its global role.[10] Today, the rules-based international order is not intended to limit US–China competition; as we will see, the rules are instruments of control and exclusion. The writing of exclusionary rules is part of the competition, not a way to avoid it.

Chapter 3 examines the AUKUS agreement, signed by the leaders of Australia, the United Kingdom and the United States. It examines the centrepiece of the agreement: the announcement that Australia will acquire at least eight nuclear-powered submarines. It discusses how AUKUS entrenches interoperability with US and UK forces. Interoperability is central to the Australian way of war: to operate inside the strategy of a superpower by contributing a well-chosen, niche capability to augment the larger force. AUKUS is the armed equivalent of the economic agreements Australia has signed with the USA and UK. It reflects a full-spectrum search for relevance to great power allies in the competition to create a new international order.

Chapter 4, 'The China divide', shows how China has become an ideological, military and economic challenger to the US-led order. It looks at the Chinese leadership's own understanding of its actions. It asks why it sees itself in that way and how those understandings have changed over time. The chapter engages with a few urgent questions facing Australia in the new era of strategic competition: What are the Chinese government's ambitions? What are its intentions? What kind of challenge does it pose?

Chapter 5, 'Expertise, secrecy and ideology', addresses questions that often come up in discussions about international relations: what does it mean to be an 'expert' in international relations, foreign affairs, national security, or politics more generally? It argues that no special qualifications are required to understand these topics. The way to proceed is to plunge in, follow leads that seem informative, try to refute your hunches, identify patterns and long-term continuities, account for what appear to be counterexamples, and work cooperatively with others to get a sense of the bigger picture. Hard work is needed, certainly, but there is nothing in politics beyond the intellectual capacities of the average person. The chapter also looks at the secrecy surrounding Australia's foreign and defence policies. The *New York Times* reported that 'Australia may well be the world's most secretive democracy'. It said that 'even among its peers, Australia stands out. No other developed democracy holds as tight to its secrets.'[11] This secrecy helps the Australian government avoid a robust, evidence-based debate as to how the defence force and intelligence services should be used. But that is hardly national security in any meaningful sense. The chapter also explores the question of whether the policy planners really believe their own rhetoric. It finds, not surprisingly, that they believe what they need to believe in order to implement the policy.

1

A subimperial power

IN SEPTEMBER 2021, THE leaders of Australia, Great Britain and the United States announced that Australia would acquire at least eight nuclear-powered submarines equipped with long-range land attack Tomahawk missiles. The announcement was part of a new trilateral security partnership known as AUKUS (Australia, the United Kingdom and the United States). AUKUS involves an increased British and American presence in Australia to support military activities in all domains: air, space, maritime, land and cyber. Australia also announced that it would scrap a $90 billion program to build French-designed diesel-powered submarines. The three countries explained that their focus was on 'interoperability' and ensuring a greater US military presence in Australia.[1] There was media commentary about the reaction in France, the cost of the submarines, how long they would take to arrive, and what China's reaction might be—but the governments' point about interoperability was largely overlooked. Yet this was perhaps the most revealing aspect of the announcement.

The overriding importance of interoperability has deep historical roots. Even before World War I, Australia rejected the Canadian Ross rifle in favour of the British Lee–Enfield as the standard weapon for the Australian military. As a military historian recounts, the Canadian weapon was 'a superlative hunting and marksman's rifle. The craftsmanship employed in machining its components was exquisite.'[2] But the Lee–Enfield was sturdy, 'accurate enough' and, most importantly, was 'the pattern adopted by the Imperial Army'.[3] That was crucial. Although the defence minister in 1909 was 'an unashamed advocate for Australian independence', he 'nevertheless recognised the need for interoperability even before the Great War'.[4] There was no contradiction between these positions. Britain was the greatest imperial power of its time, and Australia was a self-governing dominion in that empire. An imperial consciousness was intrinsic to Australian identity.

Australian foreign affairs and defence officials aimed to keep Britain involved as an imperial power in the region. Imperial force kept the colonies subjugated, their captive economies designed to make Britain rich. In turn, Britain invested its riches in Australia, developing rather than exploiting it, and laying the basis for Australian capitalism. British investors dominated foreign investment in Australia, whose economy was integrated into Britain's; more than half of Australia's exports went there, and about three-fifths of Australia's imports came from there.[5] At Federation in 1901, Australians were almost exclusively British: as many as one in five had been born in the British Isles, and almost everyone else was descended from British or Irish immigrants.[6] Australia remained the second most English country in the world even as it entered the twenty-first century.[7] Australians regarded European rule over Asian colonies as the norm: Britain in India, France in Indochina, the Netherlands in Indonesia, Portugal in East Timor. There was little interest in or support for national liberation campaigns in the colonies. Indeed, Australian leaders wanted their own colonies—Papua New Guinea and Nauru—and a combined military and economic area of influence over Fiji, Solomon Islands and Vanuatu.[8]

Australia is a different place today in many ways. Immigration patterns have changed: Australia's population now contains people from nearly every country in the world. The English are still the largest group of overseas-born people living in Australia, but those born in India and China are in second and third place respectively.[9] Constitutional amendments have placed political power firmly in the hands of Australia's own government but some features from a century ago are still present. Australian foreign policy still aims to keep a great power involved in the region. It still seeks maximum influence in the south-west Pacific and Timor-Leste. Interoperability—with the United States more than with Britain—remains a core feature of Australia's military procurement, taking precedence over other goals such as defence self-reliance and cost. The commanding general of the United States Army in the Pacific spoke of Australian forces becoming not just interoperable but also 'interchangeable': 'similar attack aviation, similar lift aviation, similar ground combat vehicles, similar air defence, short-range, long-range, similar fires, networks'.[10]

Submarines and ships are more than military platforms. They are also tools of diplomacy, indicating solidarity with allies and other like-minded countries. They add ballast to the conventional diplomatic activities carried out by Australia's Department of Foreign Affairs and Trade (DFAT). They are an instrument of statecraft: how a state uses what it has to get what it wants. The Australian government has many instruments of statecraft at its disposal: military instruments such as combat forces, joint exercises and alliance relationships; economic instruments such as trade and investment agreements; financial instruments such as international monetary agreements and foreign aid; ideological instruments such as public diplomacy campaigns; covert instruments such as espionage and other forms of intelligence; and others. Policy-makers usually explain that the aim of Australia's statecraft is a rules-based international order. We therefore examine what that phrase means.

An imperial system

Today we live in a world of independent nation-states rather than empires and colonies. The flag of the Netherlands no longer flies over Indonesia nor the Portuguese flag over Timor-Leste. But an imperial system remains in place. An empire is 'a relationship, formal or informal, in which one state controls the effective political sovereignty of others'.[11] Physical occupation is not the only way to control another country's sovereignty. Control can be established by political collaboration between both countries' elites, by economic, social or cultural dependence, by intelligence operations and by the threat of force. Julius Caesar, who knew something about empires, was quite explicit about control being more significant than annexing territory. In his *Conquest of Gaul*, he described using military force outside the formal borders of the Roman Empire to compel a tribe to act in Rome's imperial interests. Actual occupation by Caesar's legions was unnecessary if a tribe gave up its effective political sovereignty, for example by agreeing to conduct its internal affairs or its relations with other tribes in a manner approved by Rome.[12] William V. Harris, a leading scholar of classical Greco-Roman civilisation, observed that Romans usually thought of their empire '*not* as being the area covered by the formally annexed provinces, but rather as consisting of all the places over which Rome exercised power'.[13] The Roman Empire was 'the area of Roman power, not limited to the provinces'.[14]

The British Empire's senior officials also understood the crucial significance of control rather than direct colonisation. When World War I ended, they sought control of Iraq's vast oilfields, which were 'the greatest prize, perhaps the richest of the war'. Lord Curzon, a key war strategist, explained that 'there should be no actual incorporation of conquered territory in the dominions of the conqueror', but 'the absorption may be veiled by constitutional fictions as a protectorate, a sphere of influence, a buffer State, and so on'.[15]

The British Empire was different from the Roman one in many ways. The most important difference was in the nature of the imperial centre. Roman imperialism occurred centuries before the era of capitalism. It involved exploitation but few economic and social changes. People in the conquered territories continued to produce the same foodstuffs and handicrafts in the same way as before but for a foreign ruling group. By contrast, the British Empire expanded in the era of industrial capitalism. It radically transformed the territories it conquered owing to its technological, economic and political power.

The United States absorbed the lessons of the British Empire and adapted them for the post-colonial world. It recognised that British statecraft aimed at preventing European integration under a single military and economic power. Britain saw itself as an island off the coast of Europe, projecting power and influence in order to preserve a division of power there. The United States saw itself as an island off the coast of Eurasia, preserving a division of power across the Eurasian land mass.[16] Veteran naval affairs analyst Ronald O'Rourke, who also refers to this policy as 'preventing the emergence of regional hegemons', emphasises that 'US policy-makers do not often state explicitly in public' that this is the goal, but US military operations 'appear to have been carried out in no small part in support of this goal'.[17]

The North Atlantic Treaty Organization (NATO) gave the United States a dominant influence in Western Europe and ensured the primacy of a North Atlantic power system over any independent European initiatives. As NATO's secretary-general explained to President Trump, who had complained about the costs of NATO, the system 'helps the United States to project power to the Middle East, to Africa … The military clout of Europe, the economical clout, the political clout also is helpful dealing with Russia.'[18] NATO allows the US to project force against the Eurasian land mass from the west. Its military alliances with Japan and South Korea allow it to project force against that land mass from the east. The United States sees Taiwan as an 'unsinkable aircraft carrier' at the centre of an island chain off the Chinese coast.[19]

The Cold War might have ended in 1991 but NATO still preserves a division of power in Eurasia. Military bases in Japan and South Korea still allow the United States to threaten the Eurasian land mass from East Asia. And Taiwan remains what a senior US military planner called 'a critical node within the first island chain … from the Japanese archipelago down to the Philippines and into the South China Sea … anchoring a network of US allies and partners'.[20] The United States remains an island off the coast of Eurasia, projecting power from Western Europe and East Asia into the Eurasian land mass. It is the only country whose military is designed to leave its own hemisphere, cross vast oceans and airspace, and then conduct sustained, large-scale military operations in another hemisphere. This imperial objective is why the US Navy has eleven aircraft carriers while most other countries have no more than one or two; it aims at influencing the entire land mass from Portugal to Japan, from Russia's Arctic coast to India, as well as all the fringing islands such as the United Kingdom and Ireland, Sri Lanka, archipelagic south-east Asia and Japan.

As the crisis in Ukraine shows, the United States possesses overwhelming power in multiple domains. Its infrastructural power is unrivalled: it can order its near-monopoly tech giants to remove any information and expel undesirable entities from their platforms. If it chooses, it can order them to stop supplying, maintaining or updating their software in targeted countries. No other country can influence the international narrative like it, since US news agencies and wire services and its film industry set the agenda and shape perceptions. Its power over the dollar–Wall Street–IMF regime allows it to apply unilateral sanctions to weaken countries and lock them out of the dollar-denominated global financial system.[21] The Society for Worldwide Interbank Financial Telecommunication (SWIFT) is based in Brussels but with a data centre in Virginia. It allows the United States to surveil cross-border fund flows and then police them in New York, where 95 per cent of the world's dollar payments are irrevocably settled. The Clearing House Interbank Payments System (CHIPS) is a private club of forty-three financial institutions with a pre-funded account at the US Federal Reserve. They settle $1.8 trillion in claims every day and are subject to US law, allowing the United States to impose billions of dollars in fines on banks that disobey sanctions, whether legally authorised by the UN Security Council or unilaterally by the United States.[22]

Today the United States sits at the apex of a hierarchically structured imperial system, where it can control the political sovereignty of many countries without annexing them. This control is achieved via the instruments of imperial statecraft: the threat or use of military force, *coups d'état*, intelligence operations, diplomacy, trade agreements and investment treaties. Defence minister Peter Dutton made an important point when he warned that China sees Australia as a 'tributary state'. It does not wish to occupy us, he said, but rather wanted us to 'refrain from making sovereign decisions and acting in [our] self-interest'.[23] In today's imperialism, a tributary state subordinates its sovereignty to an imperial state. It makes its resources available to the imperial power in the manner desired by that power's dominant corporations. Countries that resist can be pressured, disadvantaged, excluded from key arrangements, and sometimes sanctioned, invaded or their governments overthrown in a coup.

Dutton's remarks unintentionally illustrate the magnitude of US imperial power. A comprehensive study showed that the United States tried to change other nations' governments seventy-two times during the Cold War, with sixty-six covert operations and six overt ones.[24] It did not target a single monarchy in this period; 28 per cent of covert operations targeted democracies. Covert regime change has long-term effects; the study concluded: 'States targeted for regime change were frequently less democratic afterward and more likely to experience a civil war or episode of mass killing compared to similar countries where the United States had not intervened.'[25] There is no contradiction between the professed commitment of the United States to a rules-based international order and its practice of international subversion: US policy planners understand that the rules-based international order is an imperial one.

The United States does not enforce the international order by itself. Britain supports it in various ways. The United States referred to Britain as 'our lieutenant' but noted that 'the fashionable word is partner'.[26] As the former imperial power, Britain retains a number of far-flung possessions that allow it and the United States to project power and influence: territories on which signals intelligence facilities can be installed; tax havens such as the Cayman Islands, Bermuda, Jersey, Guernsey, the Turks and Caicos Islands and the British

Virgin Islands; part of Cyprus, from which it can reach the Middle East; the Mediterranean Sea choke point of Gibraltar; the Falkland Islands; and Indian Ocean islands, which contain the Diego Garcia military base. Australia fits into this imperial system as a subimperial power. It has its own imperial area in Timor-Leste and the south-west Pacific while deploying its military and intelligence assets in defence of the US-led imperial system.

After World War II, Australia joined Britain and the United States in confronting the waves of Asian nationalism in Korea, Malaya, Vietnam and Indonesia. It aimed to defeat revolutionary social transformation among former colonies and to instal local regimes that were formally independent but economically subordinated to Western interests. Native leaders who left colonial social institutions and class relationships intact were accepted by the West, including Australia. They did not challenge local or foreign vested interests in landholdings, plantations, banks, railways, mines, businesses or government debt arrangements. But the West, including Australia, used military force, economic strangulation and intelligence operations against native leaders who wanted a new social and political order. The desired order was an imperial one: former colonies achieved formal independence but would remain subservient to the interests of private investors in crucial ways. The euphemism for this structure is a 'rules-based international order', as chapter 2 explains.

Australia is not a victim of this imperial order but a junior partner and enthusiastic—if anxious—supporter. It is not anxious because the imperial system involves frequent warfare but because it fears that the imperial centre is not sufficiently attentive to Australia. Australia has derived considerable benefits from its role in upholding the imperial system. One benefit is being a prosperous country that attracts immigrants from around the world. People *want* to come here. The Human Flight and Brain Drain Indicator measures the movement of economically productive people around the world: entrepreneurs, intellectuals and other skilled workers such as doctors, scientists and so on. It includes both voluntary emigration and forced displacement. It finds that Australia has the world's highest influx of foreign brains per capita, ahead of Sweden, Norway, Switzerland and Canada.[27] Australia also performs very high on the Human Development Index; its citizens generally enjoy long and healthy lives, are well educated, and have high living standards.

It is not surprising that Australian public opinion supports this state of affairs. For decades, opinion polls have shown strong support for Australia's alliance with the United States. The 2021 Lowy Institute poll showed three out of every four Australians believing that 'Australians and Americans share many common values and ideals. A strong alliance is a natural extension of this … the United States would come to Australia's defence if Australia was under threat'.[28] Australian public opinion contrasts sharply with global public opinion: in 2021, a poll commissioned by the Alliance of Democracies Foundation showed that nearly half (44 per cent) the 50,000 respondents in fifty-three countries surveyed were concerned that the United States threatens democracy in their country; 38 per cent feared Chinese influence.[29] In contrast, a majority of Australians (63 per cent) now see China as 'more of a security threat to Australia'.[30]

Identity informs public opinion. During the Suez Crisis of the 1950s, Australia's prime minister Robert Menzies assured Britain's Anthony Eden that 'You must never entertain any doubts about the British quality of this country'.[31] Menzies' Cabinet contained men who were born in the 1890s and the 1900s, when the British Empire reigned supreme. For them, as one historian noted, 'Australians were Britons just as their cousins at home were Britons.'[32] Identity did not operate by itself; Britain's cultural influence (via film, television and literature) and economic influence were two sides of the same coin. In the 1950s, Britain supplied 60 per cent of the total foreign investment in Australia, more than double the investment of the United States.[33] Today, the United States is the biggest investor by far and its cultural influence is overwhelming. Thus, more than three-quarters of Australians say they 'share many common values and ideals' with Americans and that 'a strong alliance is a natural extension of this'.[34] Prime Minister Julia Gillard gave voice to this sentiment when she said, 'For my own generation, the defining image of America was the landing on the moon. My classmates and I were sent home from school to watch the great moment on television. I'll always remember thinking that day: Americans can do anything ... Americans inspired the world of my own youth.'[35]

Australian policy planners today remain wedded to a 'rules-based international order'. The phrase itself is Australian, and it was intended to refer to China from the very beginning. Kevin Rudd used it in a speech in Washington DC in 2008, as the global financial crisis unfolded. He said, 'We look to China to make a strong contribution to strengthening the global and regional rules-based order.'[36] Two years later, he issued a joint statement with US Secretary of State Hillary Clinton, who was the first US Cabinet official to use that term.[37] The preference for the existing order has deep geopolitical roots.

Australia as a subimperial power

Australia was founded in the aftermath of the world's first truly global struggle, the Seven Years' War (1757–63). The claim that Australia was founded as a dumping ground for convicts is now recognised as simplistic. Britain, the greatest imperial power of its era, understood the importance of global sea power in achieving supremacy in international trade. Military historian Jeffrey Grey explains that Britain welcomed the chance to establish an intermediary port to support its trade with India and China. New Zealand and Norfolk Island had plentiful stocks of timber and flax, useful for naval vessels. It also needed a naval base from where it might interdict French, Dutch and Spanish maritime communications during wartime. Convicts would come in handy as expendable labour. A penal colony was needed after the loss of the American colonies, but the Australian colonies 'owed their foundation in large measure to the strategic perspectives in Whitehall'.[38] European settlement in Australia therefore had a subimperial dimension from its very beginning: subordinate to the imperial centre but able to project considerable power and influence in its own region.

The notion of Australia as a 'middle power' has been 'one of the most enduring themes in Australian foreign policy discourse' for seventy-five years.[39] Foreign minister Gareth Evans liked the term. So did Kevin Rudd. Julie Bishop preferred 'top twenty country' because to be in the middle of more than 180 countries 'makes us like the ninety-something country'.[40] Alexander Downer accused Labor of having 'a middle child complex when it comes to our place in the world' because Australia is not 'middling' or 'average' but 'a considerable power and a significant country'—the sixth largest country by land mass, the thirteenth largest economy, the eighth richest nation in per capita terms, the sixth oldest continuously operating democracy.[41] Statistics like these are helpful, but they do not establish whether Australia is a middle power or a considerable power or a subimperial power. Picking a term according to your personal preference does not shed much light on reality. The task is to define a term within the context of an explanatory framework. That is, what is the explanatory framework—the set of principles, assumptions and problems—within which that term is introduced? Then we ask whether the term and framework offer useful insights about Australia.[42]

To explain Australia's external relations accurately, a term must have explanatory adequacy across a wide range of phenomena. It must account for Australia's unique economic character. It must account for how Australia engages with international law, human rights, regional diplomacy, arms control, military deployments and weapons purchases. It must also account for the domestic political structures that enable those external relations. The explanatory framework of imperialism focuses on the control of other countries' sovereignty. As we have seen, control does not require physical occupation or annexation of territory. It can be established by political collaboration between both countries' elites, by economic, social or cultural dependence, by intelligence operations, or by the threat or use of force. Within this framework, Australia is a subimperial power: it is subordinate to the imperial centre, defends the imperial order known as a rules-based international order, and projects considerable power and influence in its own region.

A subimperial economy

Subimperialism accounts for Australia's unique economic character. Australia has a wealthy but dependent economy. During the colonial period, British investment fostered vertical economic ties with London more than horizontal economic ties integrating the economies of the Australian colonies. Typically found in imperial–colonial relationships, such vertical economic relationships result in monoculture economies that produce mineral resources and agricultural goods for export. That legacy remains with us.

Australia is an anomaly among advanced economies. We focus on economic growth rather than economic development. Joseph Schumpeter explained the distinction almost a century ago. Economic development, he wrote, involves 'only such changes in economic life as are not forced upon it from without but arise by its own initiative, from within'. But if an economy is 'dragged along by the changes in the surrounding world' and adapts itself to them, then there is economic growth without economic development.[43] The distinction is captured in modern economics by the concept of economic complexity. Complexity increases with a country's level of diversification (the number of products it exports). It decreases with ubiquity (the number of countries exporting the same product).[44] A country's level of economic development is associated with its economic complexity.

Australia has the lowest complexity of all the OECD countries. In 1980, Australia was ranked the fifty-first most complex economy in the world; in 2017, it was fifty-ninth. The lowest point was in 2014, when it fell to eighty-ninth.[45]

According to the chief economist in the Department of Industry, Innovation and Science, 'Australia's economic complexity is an anomaly among advanced economies, with the economic complexity closer to that of a developing country.' Australia is 'comparable to the economies of Kazakhstan, Cambodia, Kenya and Saudi Arabia'.[46] Australia's exports remain highly specialised in a few products such as iron ore, coal briquettes, gold, petroleum gas and wheat, which are typically produced by many other countries. The result is a wealthy but dependent economy.

As Paul Hasluck remarked, 'Any country has a foreign policy so that its domestic policy can be put into effect.'[47] And domestic policy reflects the fact that vital sectors of the Australian economy are integrated into the value chains of US corporations. According to data from the Bloomberg Professional Terminal, foreign investors own as much as three-quarters of the shares in the top twenty companies on the Australian Stock Exchange (ASX). These twenty companies make up approximately half the market capitalisation of the entire ASX. US-based investors are the biggest owners of sixteen of the top twenty companies.[48] As owners of the equity, they determine the corporations' priorities and practices. You cannot have an independent foreign policy when you have a dependent economy. Australia advances its economic interests—more precisely, the interests of its dominant business sectors—by working under the auspices of the United States to create an integrated global economy that offers a benign environment for international investors as well as the specific needs of key Australian corporations. The prosperity of elite Australian investors is underwritten by the same conditions that ensure the prosperity of elite US investors. In certain sectors, their fortunes are connected.

Sovereignty curtailed by the rules-based imperial order

In 2021, the Senate Economics Committee delivered a report to parliament on the regulation of foreign investment in Australia. Among other things, it examined whether there should be a positive national interest test: should prospective foreign investors be required to demonstrate how their investment would benefit Australia? If they promise that their investment will result in more jobs, a better environment, community benefits or some other advantages, can Australia make such undertakings legally enforceable? The Economics Committee asked this question to the Department of Foreign Affairs and Trade and the Office of International Law in the Attorney-General's Department. These departments 'initially declined to provide a substantive answer to these questions'. The Economics Committee 'reaffirmed its request [but] the departments responded in a manner that was not helpful'. Eventually, the committee concluded that the Australian government 'is likely prevented by international trade obligations' from requiring foreign investors to show how their investments would benefit Australia. It cannot do anything to compel foreign investors to 'carry through with the promises they make when they propose an investment'.[49]

This powerlessness implies that Australia, like many other countries, has entered into trade agreements that give a higher priority to the interests of private investors than to its own sovereignty. And on the Australian Stock Exchange, as we have seen, the dominant private investors are US-based. This is the essence of an imperial order: state sovereignty is subordinated to the interests of private investors, who can count on the support of their own powerful home states to create and preserve that order.

These investors operate in a world of global value chains (GVCs) in which the headquarters and design and engineering departments are established in one country, the manufacturing facilities in another country, and the finance and sales departments in yet another country.[50] GVCs are the dominant international corporate pattern today. An estimated 80 per cent of all international trade is simply the movement of intermediate goods and services between different arms of the same company but across international borders.[51] As the US Embassy reported in leaked diplomatic cables, Australia's automobile exports to South Korea are 'largely intra-General Motors trade to Hyundai'.[52] Australia's aircraft manufacturing and repair services exports to the United States are largely for internal components of Boeing 787 Dreamliner aircraft.[53] That is why Boeing's largest workforce outside the United States is in Australia. Australia's policy objective for the past forty years has been to integrate its economy into the world of GVCs, focusing on economic growth rather than economic development. This suits many foreign investors because they have no inherent motive to improve Australia's economic complexity.

Subimperialism in the Constitution

Subimperialism also explains Australia's reluctant, fragmented and gradual path to independence. Britain established its Australian colonies, ruled them from Britain through British officials, and populated them with Britons subject to British authority.[54] Australia's Constitution in 1901 reflected this economic tie to Britain. It 'created a free trade zone inside a customs union. A later generation might have called it the Australian Common Market.'[55] The Constitution shielded British investors from the decisions of the Australian parliament, exempting British ships in Australian waters from the application of Australian laws unless their port of clearance and port of destination were both in Australia. It included a right of appeal from Australian law courts to the Privy Council in London.[56] When the British parliament passed the Statute of Westminster in 1931, giving up control over the Australian parliament, four Australian prime ministers delayed in adopting it. Not until 1942 would the Australian parliament pass the Statute of Westminster Adoption Act.[57] Terms like 'middle power' or 'considerable power' simply cannot account for these features—but 'subimperial power' can.

Subimperialism explains why Australia's parliament and courts are excluded from national security policy. There is no Australian equivalent of the US War Powers Resolution of 1973, which places limits on the US president's freedom to order military action. The prime minister can send the Australian Defence Force into expeditionary operations overseas without parliamentary approval. There is no requirement even to debate the decision before it is announced. The power to send troops into conflict is part of the executive power set out in section 61 of the Constitution. Reform is possible; as the High Court of Australia said, parliament can 'limit or impose conditions on the exercise of the Executive power'.[58] But Australian governments have excluded parliament from authorising military deployments so that they can deploy forces abroad without political obstruction—what others might call democratic input. The term 'middle power' does not explain this but subimperialism does. Middle powers such as Norway and the Netherlands insist on parliamentary authorisation, but Australia does not.

In 1999 the Joint Standing Committee on Treaties reviewed the Australia–United States agreement to extend the operation of Pine Gap for another decade. It asked for permission to visit Pine Gap and receive an on-site, confidential briefing. The defence minister refused, saying that access was 'tightly controlled' and 'limited strictly to personnel with a "need to know"'. Instead, he offered the committee a briefing in Canberra by senior officials from his department. The committee later described the information it received in these briefings as 'assertions with little explanation or justification'. It said that this was 'not an inadvertent outcome. It resulted from a conscious decision' by senior Defence officials, 'apparently endorsed by the Minister, to limit the amount of information provided to the Committee'. Indeed, the minister later confirmed that 'none of the information provided to the Committee was classified'. Adding insult to injury, the committee learnt that 'certain members of the United States Congress have much freer access to information about the Joint Defence Facility, indeed access to the facility itself, than Australian parliamentarians'.[59] Reforms since that report have not changed the central feature of those facilities: with bipartisan support in Australia, the Australian parliament remains less aware of their activities than the US Congress. Australian strategic planners are motivated by a higher objective: upholding US imperial power.

Even the Parliamentary Joint Committee on Intelligence and Security (PJCIS) has its powers severely curtailed. The *Intelligence Services Act 2001* prevents it from 'reviewing the intelligence gathering and assessment priorities' or 'reviewing particular operations that have been, are being or are proposed to be undertaken' by the intelligence agencies, and likewise 'the sources of information, other operational assistance or operational methods' available to the agencies.[60] The PJCIS can review only the administration and financing of the intelligence agencies. The prime minister exercises a veto on who can be appointed to the PJCIS.

By contrast, the US Congress exerts its powers in full:

> Congressional oversight of the intelligence community is spread across several committees, including specialised committees on intelligence in the House of Representatives and the Senate. While each Congressional committee has some limits on what it may examine, taken collectively committees have long enjoyed the ability to

> inquire into all of the intelligence-related activities of the US Government, including highly sensitive operational matters. Wide-ranging Congressional inquiries are accepted by the US intelligence community as necessary and appropriate.[61]

Some federal parliamentarians have begun calling themselves the 'wolverines'. They declare that they are ready to confront China's expanding power. The name comes from a 1984 Hollywood film, *Red Dawn*, about a group of high school football players who defeat a Soviet invasion of the United States. The Australian wolverines display stickers featuring wolf claw marks on the entrances of their parliamentary offices. The historian James Curran says, 'It is difficult to know whether to laugh or cry at this kind of juvenilia from some of the nation's elected representatives.'[62] Whatever the reaction, the more instructive point is the subimperial ideology on display: an imagined commitment to Australian security via an American pop cultural reference. The wolverines do not demand that Australia should have US-style declassification of government records, US-style oversight of intelligence agencies or US-style parliamentary authorisation of overseas military deployments. Their pro-US stance is grounded in a solid commitment to keeping Australia subimperial.

Subimperialism and Australia's foreign wars

Subimperialism explains why less than twenty-four hours after the United States said it would begin withdrawing its troops from Afghanistan, Australia said that its troops would be withdrawn as well. The central policy objective of Australia's long war in Afghanistan and its prospective role in the Taiwan Strait is the same: the desire to achieve greater relevance in the minds of US strategic planners. Military activities in Afghanistan (or Iraq, for that matter) were less important than having senior US figures visit the Australian area of operations and appreciate its contribution. In that sense, Afghanistan was a success: the Australian flag flew alongside the US flag, demonstrating Australia's contribution to the US effort.

Australian military strategists have not focused on developing an independent military strategy. Nor have they held a debate on the future character of war. The Director of War Studies at the Australian Army Research Centre, Dr Albert Palazzo, explained why:

> The force's leadership, and its intellectually minded members who would take the lead in such a debate, do not, at least as yet, see sufficient value to the organisation in conducting it; the Australian way of war does not require it. This is not a result of a lack of capacity or facilitation for debate, although these are factors; rather it is a product of the Army's vision of itself.[63]

Subimperialism explains this state of affairs; 'middle power' does not. The aim is to uphold US military dominance, hence the deliberate choice not to develop a separate Australian military strategy.

Subimperialism also explains when Australia *does not fight* expeditionary wars. This quietude occurred in the decades after Vietnam when, as a former Chief of Army said, there was 'the occasional United Nations deployment but nothing serious happened' and the Army was 'assigned the role of strategic goalkeeper against a mythical enemy that never turned up'.[64]

Australian military writers often say that the Australian Defence Force was neglected in the 1980s and 1990s. But the military instrument had done its job by then. It had suppressed Asian nationalism and channelled it into acceptable models of economic development, setting the scene for international economic integration under so-called free trade agreements. The low priority given to the military instrument of statecraft makes sense from a subimperial perspective. Military histories of Australia's wars in south-east Asia often miss this fundamental rationale because they focus only on the Defence or Foreign Affairs sections of the Cabinet papers. Since they usually omit the domestic economic considerations that motivate external policy, they cannot show how the policy is well suited to the political logic of an integrated global economy in which Australian capital strives to operate with relative freedom.

Terms like 'middle power' and 'considerable power' do not have explanatory value across such a wide range of phenomena. Subimperialism does. In principle, there is nothing wrong with calling Australia a 'middle power' or a 'lucky country' or any other term. But the test is how useful any term is. What is the explanatory framework in which the term is embedded, and what insights about Australia can be gained from that framework?

One objection to the analysis presented here is that it is too simplistic because the facts are more complex. This objection is true but irrelevant. The facts are always more complex than any description one can give. Nothing is accomplished by trying to record enormous amounts of facts and details. That is like trying to prepare a map so detailed that it is as large as the territory it is mapping. The rational way to proceed is to identify principles with explanatory force across a wide range of phenomena, follow leads that seem informative, try to refute your hunches, pursue what appear to be counterexamples, and account for the major features of Australian foreign policy.

Chapter 2 takes a closer look at the rules-based international order. It shows that the term is a euphemism for a US-led imperial system.

2

The rules-based international order

AT A HIGH-LEVEL SUMMIT between the United States and China in March 2021, the US Secretary of State said he was 'committed to leading with diplomacy to advance the interests of the United States and to strengthen the rules-based international order'. The director of China's Foreign Affairs Commission countered by saying that China and the international community upheld 'the United Nations–centred international system and the international order underpinned by international law, not what is advocated by a small number of countries of the so-called rules-based international order'.[1] This chapter examines the rules-based international order and Australia's role in it.

Australia and the first rules-based international order

There was no need for euphemisms when James Cook claimed the eastern portion of the Australian continent for the British

Crown in 1770; the British Empire was called just that. Cook sailed up the east coast of Australia in the same year that the British East India Company's activities caused 'the loss of at least one-third of the inhabitants of the province' of Bengal, or 10 million deaths from starvation, according to its governor, Warren Hastings.[2] The British parliament, nearly a quarter of whose members held East India Company stock, backed it with state power, spending vast sums on naval and military operations to protect its acquisitions.[3] It began exporting Indian opium to China in the same year.

Two decades later, Britain's Australian colonies benefited from the subjugation of Bengal. The colony at Sydney Cove came close to starvation because its supply ship, *Guardian*, sank. Supplies of rice, semolina, lentils, clothing, livestock and seeds from Bengal in June 1792 provided a lifeline.[4] Soon, two ships a year came with supplies from India, and by 1840 a ship travelled between India and Australia approximately every four and a half days. The imperial connection saw army personnel, administrators, merchants and others moving between India and Australia.[5]

The Australian colonies prospered under the umbrella of British imperial power. They were the largest recipients of British foreign investment in the economic boom of the 1870s and 1880s.[6] That investment, in turn, came from the drain of wealth from the colonies. Between 1765 and 1938, Britain drained from India an estimated $18 trillion (£9 trillion), or ten times the United Kingdom's annual GDP today.[7] Britain sent about 45 per cent of its foreign investments to North America and Australasia between 1865 and 1914.[8] Australia, Canada and New Zealand benefited; they were among the nations that devoted the highest proportion of their incomes to education and investment in public works.[9] Meanwhile, Indian income collapsed by half and average life expectancy dropped by a fifth from 1870 to 1920.[10]

Australian leaders were committed to British control of India. Even before he became prime minister, Alfred Deakin wrote that India 'has been won by the sword, is still held by the sword, and can only be retained by the sword ... What is certain is not only that there must always be a supremacy in India, but that it must be the supremacy of arms.'[11] Commentators who refer to a shared history in order to advocate closer India–Australia ties might not be aware of what that history really was.

In the late nineteenth and early twentieth centuries, Fiji, Papua New Guinea, Solomon Islands and Vanuatu came under Australia's economic control. The Sydney-based Colonial Sugar Refining Company (CSR), for example, benefited from Fiji's sugar plantations to become the largest public company in Australia.[12] Those plantations were worked by 'coolie' labour: illiterate, vulnerable people imported from India on the basis of 'contracts' of long-term indenture. Many were seized and sent to colonial plantations forcibly, but hundreds of thousands went because the alternative was to starve during the famines under British rule. It is with good reason that a study of indentured labour was titled *A New System of Slavery*.[13]

Some wealthy Indian merchants and native princes aligned themselves with the British Empire. They benefited from this rules-based order, collaborating with the empire against their own domestic enemies. Some received properties confiscated by the British authorities. As Claude Markovits observes, 'A number of present-day Indian fortunes have their origin in the collaboration in the repression of the uprising' of 1857–58.[14] Some elite Indian families also derived their wealth from the opium trade; the British addicted the Chinese with Indian crops.[15]

Australian security under this system meant much more than the military defence of Australia. It meant a commitment to upholding the empire, which guaranteed the Australian colonies' economic interests even as it reinforced a subimperial national identity. The empire prioritised the rights of private investors over the sovereignty of conquered regions—an essential feature of that era's 'rules-based international order'. This view of security has deep roots in Australia's geopolitical tradition. Australia was part of 'Greater Britain', a multi-continental network of settler colonies that preserved the empire's geopolitical, economic and cultural strength in a world of increasing competition, particularly from Germany and the United States.[16] The imperial power and competitors are different today, but the principles are similar. Military historian Jeffrey Grey correctly observed that 'the greatest overarching myth of Australian military history' is the claim that 'Australia always fights "other people's wars"'.[17] Military historians are well aware that Australian governments have not gone to war for sentimental reasons or because they were duped. Upholding the imperial order was an essential component of Australia's security, properly understood: the security of economic interests and the military–political order that secured them. For a subimperial power, imperial wars are never 'other people's wars'.

Intellectual justifications for empire came from the most respectable liberal sources. John Stuart Mill justified Britain's conquests on humanitarian grounds. Britain, he said, acted 'rather in the service of others, than of itself'. The 'aggressions of barbarians force it to successful war', but Britain bore the costs of war while it receives the fruits 'it shares in fraternal equality with the whole human race … A nation adopting this policy is a novelty in the world; so much so it would appear that many are unable to believe it when they see it.'[18] Mill was writing in 1859, a date that is significant for two reasons: Britain was involved in the largest narco-trafficking operation in history, compelling millions of Chinese to become opium addicts through force of arms.[19] And imperial force had just crushed the Indian Mutiny of 1857–58, in which around 800,000 people were killed, although the number could well be higher.[20] Yet Mill no doubt genuinely believed in the benevolence of the empire. Charles Dickens, rightly praised for his deep sympathy for the English working class, was also an enthusiastic supporter of imperial violence in the colonies. 'I wish I were Commander in Chief in India,' he wrote. He said he would 'strike that Oriental race with amazement' and 'proclaim to them in their language' that he 'was now proceeding, with all convenient dispatch and merciful swiftness of execution, to blot it out of mankind and raze it off the face of the Earth'.[21] Imperial liberalism reconciled the quest for freedom, democracy and prosperity with the imperial interests of those with real economic power.[22]

Intellectual support for a US-led global order today has a familiar ring. Discussion of the rules-based international order assumes reflexively that the goals and motives of the United

States are noble, sincere and benign. No evidence needs to be offered because it is assumed to be true by definition. In 1967, Prince Sihanouk of Cambodia told Australian prime minister Harold Holt that the US assault on Indochina was 'essentially an example of foreign intervention in the internal affairs of an Asian country and a blatant breach of the Geneva Agreements'. The prime minister replied that whatever criticism might be levelled at the US action in Vietnam, 'it had been undertaken with the best of intentions and for the best of motives'.[23]

The assumption of benign intentions and motives occurs in all imperial systems. France's supreme military commander in Indochina in the 1950s assured Australia's foreign minister Richard Casey that he was not fighting a colonial war at all. 'There was,' he said, 'no longer an ounce of colonialism left in French intentions.' Rather, he was 'leading a crusade against Communism … Not since the Crusades has France undertaken such disinterested action.'[24] There may be errors and other ironies of history, but the motives are always assumed to be sincere. John Howard explained that despite the failure to find Iraq's weapons of mass destruction in 2003, 'it was wrong to claim the intelligence had been cooked up to justify the invasion'. He said, 'It may have been an erroneous conclusion based on the available information, but it wasn't made up.'[25] There is no need to provide facts or evidence of good intentions because the claim has the status of a theological principle.

Economics of the rules-based international order

A century before, Adam Smith had explained the economics of empire. The American colonies, he wrote in *The Wealth of*

Nations, should focus on agriculture and leave manufacturing to Britain. If the Americans were 'to stop the importation of European manufactures' in favour of 'their own countrymen as could manufacture the like goods', they would 'obstruct instead of promoting the progress of their country towards real wealth and greatness'.[26] Having defeated Britain, however, the Americans could reject his advice and construct an industrial base behind high tariff walls. The United States became the 'mother country and bastion of modern protectionism', as Paul Bairoch has shown. It imposed 'strict protectionism' from 1861 until the end of the nineteenth century, resulting in very rapid growth from 1870 to 1892, a period that 'can be regarded as among the most prosperous in the whole economic history of the United States'.[27] Had the Americans followed the principle of comparative advantage, they would be exporting furs and bison meat.

Cotton and water were the key inputs of the nineteenth century's textile-based Industrial Revolution. History is kind enough to provide a comparison: Egypt, like the southern United States, was rich in water and cotton and was in a good position to undertake rapid economic development. Its modernising leader, Mohammad Ali, had begun to build a modern military. He constructed factories and shipyards to support this endeavour and imposed state monopolies to pay for them. British leaders had other ideas. 'A manufacturing country Egypt never can become', one declared. Rather, 'by the peaceful development of her agricultural aptitude she may interest and benefit all'.[28] Imperial force ended Mohammad Ali's attempt at industrialisation and 'Egypt was relegated to the status of a province whose sole commercial and economic function was to supply raw materials for European industry', as an Egyptian historian recounts.[29]

The different fates of the United States and Egypt are a good illustration of the economics of empire. The principle of comparative advantage promoted by Adam Smith and David Ricardo, who followed him, held that specialisation and trade according to comparative costs would lead to mutual benefit. Using a two-country, two-commodity model, Ricardo said that even if Portugal could produce both cloth and wine more cheaply than England, England should still specialise in cloth and Portugal in wine because the relative costs were different; that is, England, by producing one unit less of wine, could produce more cloth than Portugal could by the same method. However, as Utsa and Prabhat Patnaik have shown, the argument contains a fatal flaw: it depends crucially on the assumption that both countries produce both goods. But Britain, unlike Egypt, could not produce sufficient cotton at home regardless of the amount of land and water used in the attempt. More generally, capitalism as it actually exists has its home base in the northern countries, which are primarily located in the temperate areas of the globe. They demand a range of goods that can be produced only in the tropical and semi-tropical regions. And that requires the subordination of those regions by military force or trade agreements—a rules-based order.

The modern version of Ricardo's view is expressed in the Heckscher–Ohlin–Samuelson model, which is based on relative endowments of 'factors of production'. It implies that countries with lots of capital equipment should specialise in capital-intensive goods while countries with lots of cheap labour should specialise in labour-intensive goods. The way to make this happen is by removing subsidies, tariffs and other 'distortions', thus allowing all countries to move naturally towards their own comparative strengths. But the reason poor countries do not have enough capital is that they were conquered and dispossessed, then subjected to unjust rules contained in unequal treaties. The reason rich countries have lots of capital is that they were imperial powers or benefited from empire, could develop their industries behind protectionist walls, and benefited from strong unions and robust labour laws.[30] In the 1860s, Japan and the Asante kingdom in West Africa were at similar developmental levels in terms of access to resources, level of state formation, and an institutional and cultural framework capable of adapting foreign technology and ideas to local conditions.[31] The Meiji Restoration (between 1868 and 1889) meant that Japan modernised and avoided being colonised. It became the only non-European country to join the First World. The Asante were not so fortunate; they became the West African colonies of the Gold Coast and Ghana. Sri Lanka exports tea in such large quantities because the colonial power's land policies converted the hill country into plantations and imported cheap labour from India to cultivate them. A political decision, in other words, not some 'natural' condition.

Belief in imperial benevolence supplied the ideological justification for empire. Comparative advantage supplied the economic justification. Military force supplied the hard power. As military historian Craig Stockings notes, Australian strategic planners recognised that 'for the Empire to be strong anywhere, it needed to be strong everywhere'. Far from being 'other people's wars', the reality is that 'Australia's wars have been Australia's choices, or at least the consequence of the willing decisions of Australian politicians and policymakers in pursuit of the perceived national interest'.[32] The organising principle of Australian foreign policy is to remain on the winning side of a worldwide confrontation between the empire and the lands dominated by it. Australia's strategic reflex is therefore to fit into the global strategy of a great power.

Australia and the second rules-based international order

This strategic reflex was on display in the *2016* Defence White Paper. Issued by the Turnbull government in the last year of the Obama administration, it exhibited a deep anxiety about the security of US power-projection capabilities in north-east Asia. It mentioned the rules-based order fifty-three times, did not mention the Asia Pacific at all but referred to the Indo-Pacific sixty-eight times. Clearly, China's rise is of deep concern to Australia's defence and security establishment, which has coasted in the slipstream of US supremacy since the end of World War II.

Their concern was heightened by President Trump's less than reflexive support for the status quo. His apparently transactional approach to his country's alliances with Japan and South Korea alarmed Australian planners, as did his initiatives to reduce the US military presence in Germany, Afghanistan and Iraq. In response, they released a White Paper on Foreign Policy in 2017. It urged a 'rules-based order' in the 'Indo-Pacific'—a region it referred to seventy-four times. Richard Maude, who led the whole-of-government taskforce involved in preparing that document, later explained that there was a 'growing worry that the United States' weight in the region was weakening compared to China's'.[33] Australia needed to be a more vocal advocate for US power in the region and to put its money where its mouth is. This is the context for the 2020 *Defence Strategic Update* and *Force Structure Plan*, launched with great fanfare by the Morrison government, and the classified *Defence Planning Guidance*. The documents show that the policy planners who determine Australian defence policy will do whatever it takes to strengthen American resolve.

Under Trump's presidency, the COVID-19 pandemic was the first major international crisis since World War II in which the United States did not act as the global leader for coordinating or implementing an international response. But others in the Trump administration understood and accepted the imperial role of the United States. Secretary of State Mike Pompeo moved from containment to encirclement of China: reinforcing US forces in the Pacific, strengthening military ties with Australia, Japan, South Korea and India, increasing diplomatic ties with Taiwan, and direct criticism of China as an enemy of Western values.

The Biden administration embraced Pompeo's encirclement strategy. It announced the relocation of US marines from Okinawa to Guam, where an integrated air and missile defence system is planned. The aim is a Joint Fires Network that enables any sensor from any platform (air, land, sea, space, cyberspace) to provide targeting guidance to any weapon. In December 2021, President Biden signed the 2022 National Defence Authorization Act (NDAA) into law. Its gigantic US$768 billion program contained what one strategic analyst called 'a detailed blueprint for surrounding China with a potentially suffocating network of US bases, military forces, and increasingly militarized partner states. The goal is to enable Washington to barricade that country's military inside its own territory and potentially cripple its economy in any future crisis.'[34] Australia is part of this 'unbroken chain of US-armed sentinel states', which includes Japan, South Korea, Taiwan, the Philippines, Thailand, Singapore and India.

The Joint Defence Facility at Pine Gap in the Northern Territory makes a vital contribution to the US war-fighting mission. The base provided tactical intelligence to Australian forces when they upheld the US alliance in Afghanistan. Satellites in a space-based intelligence collection system detect and locate radio signals linked to improvised explosive devices (IED). Known as the Red Dot system, it integrates signals, imaging and all-source inputs in order to place a red dot on a computer display in a vehicle, alerting friendly forces to the existence of a possible IED ahead.[35] Operational since at least 1970, it integrates Australia into US war-fighting machinery.

The cover story is that it contributes to nuclear deterrence and arms control agreements by providing timely information on missile launches and nuclear tests. But, as Brian Toohey has shown, the truth is that 'the central figure for arms control agreements' is the total number of missiles and warheads, which is verified by photographic images from low-orbiting satellites. Pine Gap contributes 'next to nothing' because its satellites 'only provide information about ... particular [missiles] tested'. Instead, the facility acquires information from US satellites detecting heat from aircraft, artillery, missiles, drones and space vehicles, as well as military and civilian communications. The data is processed into usable intelligence and employed against those whom the United States considers hostile. Pine Gap is therefore 'essentially irrelevant to verifying compliance with arms control agreements'.[36]

Australia's official position is 'full knowledge and concurrence'. In 2013, defence minister Stephen Smith explained what that phrase meant. He said that 'full knowledge' meant having a full and detailed understanding of any US capability or activity with a presence on Australian territory or making use of Australian assets. Australia conducts an annual full knowledge and concurrence audit, which includes 'the systems' bandwidth, data rates and information collected, the type and function of communications transmitted, proposed changes to its usage, and an understanding of the totality of the system and the uses to which it may be put'.[37] Smith explained that 'concurrence' meant Australia approved the presence of a US capability or function in Australia in support of mutually agreed goals. Concurrence did not mean that Australia approved every activity or tasking undertaken.

Smith's statement shows that Australian policy planners know that the United States has an unsentimental, cynical view of power. They do not need to be told that the true character of our relationship with the United States is a transactional, dramatically unequal one. Australian diplomats strive continuously to show their relevance to American policy-makers precisely because they know how little Australia features in US thinking. The rhetoric of 'mateship' is window dressing for the public, the media and the parliament. Pine Gap is shrouded in secrecy for reasons that go well beyond protecting its technology. An important reason is that Pine Gap makes Australia a co-belligerent with the United States under international law, which states that 'a neutral State must not assist the war effort of one of the belligerents against its adversary through military supplies furnished on an intergovernmental basis'.[38] As Kim Beazley said in 2021, 'The capabilities are vastly greater than when I was Defence Minister and our integration much deeper.'[39] Secrecy prevents domestic and international debate as to Australia's co-belligerency in the wars against Libya, Syria, Yemen, Iraq, Afghanistan and wherever the United States goes to war next.

But to what end? Isn't the economic relationship with China too important to jeopardise? Why aren't Australia's mining and energy billionaires up in arms? The answer is that they take seriously the government's insistence that its highest priority is to uphold the rules-based international order—and they know that that order is the US-led imperial system, whose preservation offers greater long-term benefits to them. They know it prioritises the rights of private investors over the sovereignty of most states. They know the US-led imperial system serves as a bulwark against efforts in developing countries to control the pace, depth and terms of their integration into the international economic system dominated largely by Western investors. Otherwise they might use their resources for their own social and economic development instead of making them available under the comparative advantage system.

An imperial lens provides a more precise explanation of how the rules-based order operates and in whose interests. The rules by which other countries' sovereignty is controlled include the investor-rights treaties misleadingly called free trade agreements. They subordinate state sovereignty to the interests of private investors. On the specific question of iron-ore exports, the mining magnates understand that China has no effective alternative to Australia; the only competitor is Guinea, on the west coast of Africa. But the Simandou mine there, which has higher iron content, has yet to export a single tonne of the commodity. Developing it will require the construction of a 650-kilometre railway with multiple bridges, sidings and more than 25 kilometres of tunnels to link it to a deep-water port on the coast.[40] And then the transport costs will be higher, given the longer sea route.

It is no accident that the National Party, which enjoys the closest links to mining and trade interests, is out in front on war talk. When Barnaby Joyce was sworn in as deputy prime minister in June 2021, he issued a stark warning about China in his first speech to the Coalition party room. He said there was 'a unifying cause' that is 'more important to the nation than anything else … [W]hat is required of us is to make Australia as strong as possible as quickly as possible in order to protect our way of life.' Pointing to the electoral benefits, Joyce added that it was 'a comparative strength for the Coalition'.[41] The Morrison government's attempt to run a khaki election in 2022 reflects this point of view.

In the 1950s, the ideology of anti-communism was a political bludgeon against the parliamentary opposition and a justification to use the police and intelligence agencies against domestic constituencies. It was also a highly effective technique of mobilising the public as Australia joined the United States in defeating revolutionary social transformation among newly independent former colonies in south-east

Asia. Of course, the Chinese Communist Party's monopoly on state power is real enough. So is its authoritarianism towards those who challenge it, as people in Hong Kong, Tibet and Xinjiang can testify. What is a fiction is the pretext for which it is used: concern about self-determination for China's ethnic minorities. The loudest voices in defence of self-determination for Taiwan have little to say about Indonesia's West Papuan minority or the status of Kashmir, ruled by both Pakistan and India—until, that is, it becomes necessary to weaponise those territories against those countries.

In October 2013, three West Papuan activists tried to seek support for their cause at the Australian consulate in Bali. Their request was modest; they made no reference to independence but called for the release of political prisoners and for 'foreigners, including journalists, diplomats, observers and tourists, to be able to visit West Papua freely'.[42] Prime minister Tony Abbott rejected them, saying, 'Australia will not give people a platform to grandstand against Indonesia. People seeking to grandstand against Indonesia, please, don't look to do it in Australia. You are not welcome.'[43] Abbott resurfaced eight years later in Taiwan, grandstanding about Taiwanese self-determination.[44] Australia opposes West Papuan self-determination but backs Taiwan—or rather, the US approach to it.

In the 1950s, Australian policy-makers opposed Indonesian control of West Papua. They saw the territory as 'occupying a position of great strategic and tactical importance, guarding as it does the western approaches to Torres Strait and the northern approaches to Darwin. Its western and northern coasts particularly contain a number of first-class harbours and airfield sites.'[45] They dropped their opposition as the Cold War developed and began backing Indonesia's efforts to seize the territory. In May 1969, two young West Papuan leaders named Clemens Runaweri and Willem Zonggonau attempted to fly to New York to alert the United Nations to Indonesia's impending takeover. Australian authorities detained them on Manus Island when their plane stopped to refuel, ensuring that West Papuan voices were silenced.[46] This is not hypocrisy or double standards; it is not as though Australia is committed to self-determination as a value. Rather, policy is informed by a single standard: support for the imperial order. Self-determination is weaponised in support of that standard.

There is another reason that Australia's mining and energy corporations are not telling the government to back off: the strategic heights of these sectors are owned by US-based investors. BHP is widely known as the Big Australian but according to the Bloomberg Professional Terminal it is 71 per cent US owned. Rio Tinto is 77 per cent US owned. Woodside Petroleum is 63 per cent US owned. Newcrest Mining is 53 per cent US owned. South32, a diversified metals and mining company, is 47 per cent US owned.[47] The only mining company on the ASX that is not US majority-owned is Fortescue Metals, which Andrew 'Twiggy' Forrest controls. Dr Forrest is Australia's fourth richest person, with a net worth estimated at $16.3 billion. According to the Bloomberg news organisation, he holds a 29.8 per cent stake in Fortescue through closely held Minderoo Group and remains its chairman.[48] It is perhaps no coincidence that he has been the most visibly vocal member of his tiny class to differ from the New Cold War rhetoric.

Australia could assert greater policy autonomy over its critical minerals, especially since strategic competition will play out on a technological battlefield. In 2013, Geoscience Australia conducted a study of 'Critical commodities for a high-tech world'.[49] It found that Australia was rich in antimony, beryllium, bismuth, chromium, cobalt, copper, graphite, helium, indium, lithium, manganese, molybdenum, nickel, niobium, platinum-group elements, rare-earth elements, tantalum, thorium, tin, titanium, tungsten and zirconium. Some of these commodities are considered most critical by the European Union, Japan, South Korea, the United Kingdom and the United States. Australia could establish a nationally owned company that exercised ownership and control of strategically important minerals. It would then be in a position to increase domestic innovation and support higher value-added sectors, such as high-technology research and development, advanced manufacturing, and energy efficiency. The aim here would be to increase Australia's economic complexity by diversifying exports into higher value-added sectors. The aim would be to build horizontal economic linkages that can generate a 'spread effect', such that mining operations enable new domestic industries and workers who are trained for more highly skilled tasks.[50]

But Australia's Department of Industry is a true believer in the doctrine of comparative advantage. Its Critical Minerals Strategy is not concerned with nation-building or increasing economic complexity but with creating a permissive environment for foreign investors to carve up Australia's critical minerals. Its aim is to make Australia a better quarry. The business press reports approvingly that 'the Aussies come to

Europe's rare-earth rescue … When the EU goes looking for supplier countries for critical minerals to feed its manufacturing, several sets of ears around the world prick up at this, but few as eagerly as those in Canberra.'[51] You could say the same thing about Australia's Defence and Foreign Affairs officials, whose ears prick up just as easily—since their pursuit of relevance to the United States is the external expression of this economic dependence. As we will see in chapter 3, the Australia–United Kingdom–United States agreement (AUKUS) is the military component of the Australia–United States Free Trade Agreement (AUSFTA) and the Australia–United Kingdom Free Trade Agreement (AUKFTA).

A note of caution should be sounded, however, because extracting the minerals needed for a so-called green transition is not at all straightforward.[52] A rechargeable battery in an electric car typically contains lithium, cobalt, nickel, graphite and copper. It weighs around 450 kg but, as a Manhattan Institute study found, requires mining about 40,000 kg of ore to acquire just these five elements for a single car battery. The same study found that a single electric car requires more cobalt than a thousand smartphone batteries; the blades on just one wind turbine require more plastic than five million smartphones; and, at the current rate, by 2050 the quantity of worn-out solar panels, much of it non-recyclable, 'will constitute double the tonnage of all today's global plastic waste, along with over three million tons per year of unrecyclable plastics from worn-out wind turbine blades. By 2030, more than 10 million tons per year of batteries will become garbage.'[53] The environmental damage can result in what are called ‘sacrifice zones’: areas with severe environmental damage, potentially extending to outer space, including the Moon and other celestial bodies.

The point here is that an elite consensus combines the pursuit of relevance to the United States in foreign and defence policy with the doctrine of comparative advantage in economics. There is little evidence of ambition to develop formal industrial policies aimed at stimulating economic development and rebuilding the manufacturing base to better position Australia in advanced technology areas. Instead, as one writer quipped, it is ‘simply accepted that we will be a huge quarry/farm that ships bits of the continent north, and we’ll sell each other $7 coffees with the proceeds’.[54]

Even with all this, it is not easy to argue that the status quo genuinely harms Australians when balanced against the other benefits that flow from a liberal international trading order underpinned by US power. That order produces winners and losers; Australia is in the former group, and there is very little consideration of the interests of the latter. Until that changes, the policy rationale is unaltered.

The other subimperial power

As an active, eager participant in the US-led order, Australia plays a role similar to that played by Israel in a much more strategically critical part of the world. Australia supports its subimperial counterpart even when its actions are detrimental to Australia. In January 2010, an Israeli assassination squad killed a Palestinian man in a hotel in Dubai. Using closed circuit television footage and other evidence, the local police released the names of twenty-six suspects along with details of false passports and credit cards used in the operation. Three of the passports were Australian. Israel had violated the integrity of the Australian passport system, threatening the safety of thousands of Australians who travel in the Middle East. Security services of Middle Eastern countries—and in the wider world—would look with suspicion on innocent Australians. The foreign minister announced the expulsion of an Israeli diplomat, believed to be an intelligence officer.[55]

Years later, prime minister Kevin Rudd revealed that it was not the first time Israel had done this:

> Back in 2003, under the Howard government, the Israeli intelligence services had taken it into their heads to use forged Australian passports in one of their operations abroad. They had been found out. Dennis Richardson, the director-general of the Australian Security Intelligence Organisation at the time, had hauled them over the coals. The Israelis had been forced to sign an agreement with us that if we were to continue intelligence cooperation with them in the future, they would never do this again. Obviously the Israelis had not taken us seriously, because they did it again.[56]

Australia's national security establishment might have been genuinely angry but Australia continued to support Israel at the United Nations. The US Embassy discussed the matter with an Australian diplomat in DFAT's Middle East Section. The diplomat assured the United States that the 'harsh rhetoric' notwithstanding, Australia would not vote for a UN General Assembly Resolution critical of Israel.[57] In other words, the aim was to preserve the US-led imperial order and Israel was vital to that aim. Australian policy stays on the winning side of this international order, despite the internal costs involved. The interests of those on the losing side are not a concern for policy-makers.

Australian planners understand that Israel upholds a pro-US order in a critical area of the world: the Middle East, with its huge oil resources. In 1967, Israel defeated Egypt and Syria in the Six Day War, and in doing so prevented secular nationalism from becoming the leading political current in the Arab Muslim world. Instead, radical fundamentalist Islam led by Saudi Arabia emerged as the dominant current. For its part, Israel began acting as a proxy for the United States around the world: in Central America, Africa and elsewhere.[58] As Joe Biden once remarked, 'If there were not an Israel, we would have to invent one to make sure our interests were preserved.'[59] US legislation requires the preservation of a Qualitative Military Edge for Israel; any weapons sales to the Middle East require certification by the US Defense Security Cooperation Agency that '[t]he proposed sale will not alter the basic military balance in the region'.[60] Israel has an advanced economy with a cutting-edge high-tech sector in which its government plays a substantial role. It is competitive in aviation, communications, computer-aided design and manufactures, medical electronics and fibre optics.

Ideological factors also motivate support for Israel, to be sure. Christian Zionism is an important intellectual current, with its conception of biblical promises being realised. So is the common sense of being a European power in a non-European area. As Israel's ambassador to Australia once said, 'Israel and Australia are like sisters in Asia. We are in Asia without the characteristics of Asians. We don't have yellow skin and slanty eyes. Asia is basically the yellow race. Australia and Israel are not—we are basically the white race. We are on the western side of Asia and they are on the south-eastern side.'[61] The ambassador's remarks drew on a history of subimperial race consciousness, although they were expressed too crudely for modern sensibilities.

Israel has been designated an apartheid state by Human Rights Watch, Amnesty International and the Israeli Information Center for Human Rights in the Occupied Territories.[62] Australia supports Israel regardless of its conduct, but not because it has been manipulated by a domestic ethnic lobby. No lobby group in Australia can dominate foreign policy or acquire influence in the mainstream media for very long unless its goals are aligned with the broader interests of Australian capitalism. The so-called Israeli Lobby has not hijacked Australian foreign policy but operates in harmony with it. There is a strategic convergence between its aims and the 'national interest' of upholding the US-led imperial order. Similarly, the Australian government was not manipulated by a string-pulling 'Jakarta Lobby' when it supported the military dictatorship of General Suharto in Indonesia for thirty-two years. Rather, it recognised that Suharto had destroyed the prospect of social transformation in Indonesia, turning his country into a pro-Western, stable, client state. Support for client regimes and for another subimperial power is well within the mainstream of imperial history.

Australia and Timor-Leste

Australia exercises imperial power in its own area of influence: the south-west Pacific and Timor-Leste. It accepted Timor-Leste's formal independence in 2002 but blocked its economic independence. It refused to negotiate a maritime boundary along the median line in the Timor Sea. It withdrew from the maritime boundary jurisdiction of the International Court of Justice and the International Tribunal on the Law of the Sea in March 2002, ensuring that Timor-Leste, which would become independent in May 2002, could not exercise its legal rights at these forums. Australia used overt and covert methods to deny Timor-Leste sovereignty over its oil and gas resources. It ordered its spy agency, the Australian Secret Intelligence Service (ASIS), to conduct an operation against Timor-Leste. Under the cover of a foreign aid program, ASIS installed listening devices in Timor-Leste's government offices to eavesdrop on its internal discussions during oil and gas negotiations with Australia.

The Timorese government made a determined attempt to assert its legal rights. Timorese civil society protested against Australia's conduct. But the Australian government achieved its objectives despite that resistance. A treaty signed in 2018 denied Timor-Leste any compensation for Australia's past exploitation of the oil and gas fields in the Timor Sea, including those that would have rightfully gone to Timor-Leste, had a median line been drawn in 2002. The Department of Foreign Affairs and Trade called this 'an example of the rules-based order in action'.[63] DFAT's explanation confirms that there is no contradiction between Australia's professed commitment to a rules-based international order and its rich record of imperial conduct towards Timor-Leste. That is because the rules-based international order is a euphemism for imperial practice.

Australia offered technical assistance to make Timor-Leste attractive to foreign investors. It offered educational scholarships in Australia and used its alumni networks to build links with past recipients. It offered military exercises and training to create shared habits, procedures and sentiments between the Timor-Leste Defence Force and the Australian Defence Force. It influenced key aspects of Timor-Leste's domestic policies in order to help create a tiny urban middle class rather than make poverty eradication a priority. The result was poverty in the countryside that sparked migration to the capital, structural unemployment and a small urban middle class that is positively disposed to the Australian government's foreign aid initiatives and view of the world. The Australian government thus achieved most of its policy objectives in Timor-Leste. Control over Timor-Leste's sovereignty is imperialism by a different method than that carried out by Indonesia in Timor-Leste, but it is imperialism because it involved control of that country's resources and key decisions.

A force-based international order

For the imperial power and its delegates, a rules-based order is not an alternative to a force-based one. The Bush administration declared openly in 2002 that it would attack potential challengers even before they posed an immediate threat.[64] The only remarkable thing about this declaration was that it was made explicit; as a former Secretary of State wrote, 'anticipatory self-defense' is 'a tool every president has quietly held in reserve'.[65] Thus, the rules-based order permits the United States and its allies to invade Iraq illegally and attack a hospital in the city of Fallujah. It allows Saudi Arabia and the United Arab Emirates to create a humanitarian crisis in Yemen.[66]

Likewise, Indonesia's leading war criminals paid no price for their destruction of East Timor in 1999, nor for their genocidal twenty-four-year operations there. Indonesia's National Commission on Human Rights found evidence of 'systematic and mass murder, extensive destruction, enslavement, forced deportations and displacement and other inhumane acts committed against the civilian population'.[67] The UN Commission on Human Rights reported that its members 'were confronted with testimonies surpassing their imagination' in East Timor.[68] It called for an international human rights tribunal to bring the perpetrators to justice. They remain at large, enjoying successful careers in politics and commerce, and good relations with Australia. This is the rules-based international order in action.

The rules-based order

We see therefore that the rules-based order differs sharply from the United Nations–centred international system and the international order underpinned by international law. The

United States sits at the apex of the system, exercising control over the sovereignty of many countries. The United Kingdom, a lieutenant with nuclear weapons and far-flung territories, supports the United States. So do subimperial powers like Australia and Israel. The Australian public incurs costs, but much heavier costs are borne by the losers within the system: former colonies known as the Global South and others on the receiving end of imperial dominance. Australia's participation allows it to claim a division of the spoils. As one strategist said, 'The expense required to develop these capabilities can therefore be regarded as a form of investment in the capacity to influence outcomes in a coalition setting. Putting it crudely, the more Australia brings to the table, the more it is likely to be able to take away from it at the end.'[69]

The rules-based international order involves control of the effective political sovereignty of other countries, a belief in imperial benevolence and the economics of comparative advantage. Since policy planners and media commentators cannot bring themselves to say 'empire', the 'rules-based international order' serves as the euphemism.

3

AUKUS

THIS CHAPTER EXAMINES THE AUKUS agreement, signed by the leaders of Australia, the United Kingdom and the United States. AUKUS is a trilateral security agreement whose centrepiece, the exchange of naval nuclear propulsion information, is the acquisition by Australia of at least eight nuclear-powered submarines.

Why submarines

Submarines provide a vital, highly specialised capability for a maritime nation like Australia. They raise the stakes for any adversary contemplating hostile action. Anti-submarine warfare, at which Australia is adept, requires a range of costly, cutting-edge capabilities in the air and at sea, and is one of the most complex warfare disciplines to master. Submarines are expensive, but countermeasures against them are much more expensive. Submarines give Australia a strategic weight that no other Australian Defence Force (ADF) asset or combination of assets does. If Australia ever decided to have an independent foreign and defence policy, it would need to possess those capabilities. They allow the government to act at a time of its choosing and under any realistic threat scenario. These capabilities cannot be turned on quickly; they require years of investment in personnel and equipment to achieve proficiency.

Australia's proficiency in this area was shown during the East Timor crisis of 1999 when Indonesia deployed two submarines to shadow Australian and New Zealand ships taking troops, fuel and supplies to the territory. The submarines were detected and their locations signalled to higher-level headquarters in Australia. Australian commanders then contacted their Indonesian counterparts and provided convincing information to show that their actions had been detected. The appropriate Indonesian commander then 'admitted that his submarines had been deployed forward and agreed to retire them from the area', according to an account by defence strategist David Dickens.[1]

In the future it might become politically feasible to adopt a policy of armed independence rather than the subimperialism that has characterised Australian defence strategy since Federation. Such a policy would require a posture known as the 'strategic defensive': making Australian forces an aggressive, elusive military that avoids detection, seeks battle on very favourable terms, and compels a hostile adversary to abandon its goals. As Australian strategist Dr Albert Palazzo says, the

Army is already acquiring a long-range strike missile capability that enables it to create a 2,000-kilometre killing zone along the approaches to our north.[2] Submarines and anti-submarine warfare assets will complement this capability in all realistic threat scenarios, and this would be especially true under any future policy of armed independence.

These capabilities only require conventional submarines, not nuclear-powered ones. But the Royal Australian Navy has consistently preferred submarines far in excess of Australia's proximate defence needs; as one defence minister said quite bluntly, 'Ideally, we are seeking a comparable capability to a nuclear submarine with diesel-electric motors inside.'[3] Since Australia has no domestic nuclear power industry—necessary if a country is to operate nuclear-powered submarines in a self-reliant manner—it is stuck with diesel-electric boats for decades but imposes on them demands far greater than those imposed by any other non-nuclear navy. Australia's submariners are embedded in the US torpedo and combat data system program. The relationship was so close, one insider observed, that 'the first live warshot firing of the latest variant of the main US Navy heavyweight torpedo, the Mark 48 CBASS, was conducted by an Australian submarine'.[4] The AUKUS announcement implies that Australia has prioritised full interoperability with the United States. Indeed, the government has decided to host US submarines in Western Australia until Australia's own boats arrive in the 2040s—meaning, essentially, that Australia has outsourced its submarine capability to the US Navy for the next two decades.

Full interoperability means, among other things, compatibility with the US Navy's underwater surveillance system, which tracks other countries' submarines at long distances. This involves taking advantage of the sound channel, a layer in the oceans about one kilometre deep, acoustically isolated from the ocean layers above and below it. A network of underwater microphones is mounted on the seafloor at key locations in the Pacific and Atlantic oceans, recording low-frequency noise in the sound channel and transmitting it via undersea cables to shore stations for analysis. These sensing devices are also placed at choke points near China's coastline, allowing the United States to monitor Chinese ballistic-missile submarines as they try to gain access to the open ocean. The United States can send firing orders to its hunter–killer submarines via the Harold E. Holt Naval Communications Station near the town of Exmouth in Western Australia, better known as North West Cape. These submarines can trail Chinese submarines and sink them at the outbreak of hostilities, eliminating China's small nuclear deterrent. China therefore has an incentive to launch first if it believes an attack is imminent.[5] In 2008, the Rudd government signed a treaty giving the United States access to and use of North West Cape for the next twenty-five years—allowing it to be used in a nuclear war, if things go that far.

There have been suggestions that the submarines are needed because they protect Australia's access to energy and other materials in which Australia is not self-sufficient. While it is true that Australia needs imports and uses the seas rather than land to transport them, China's energy flows are even more vulnerable. It is the world's largest importer of oil and relies on imports to meet almost 75 per cent of its consumption. It is also one of the world's largest natural gas importers, relying on imports to meet more than 40 per cent of its domestic needs.[6] It has to confront what former president Hu Jintao called the 'Malacca dilemma': most of its energy imports have to pass through the Strait of Malacca after making the long transit across the Indian Ocean, which is heavily patrolled by increasingly hostile navies. A war in the western Pacific would disrupt nearly all Chinese trade. International shipping and air transport companies would not enter the combat zone because they would rather lose revenue than ships and aircraft.

Australian planners are not driven by strangulation scenarios, although they might use them to justify a policy that has other motives. There is a word for these threat scenarios: projection. If the objective is to join the United States in threatening China's fuel supplies, such a policy cannot be stated quite so brazenly. It must be recast in terms of threat: a communist government bent on world domination, in which disputes over exclusive economic zones and Taiwan are ultimately the forward elements of an international totalitarian wave. In fact, AUKUS provides evidence for a different conclusion; namely, that it is a conscious application of principles of imperial planning that long pre-date the current period.

Exclusive economic zones and power projection

Nuclear-powered submarines will help Australia enforce the United States' self-defined right to project power globally under the guise of 'freedom of navigation'. There is a popular misconception about this matter, recently illustrated in the ABC television comedy *Utopia*. One episode satirises

Australian defence policy by saying that increased military spending is intended to protect our shipping routes. Since China is our major trading partner, and in that scenario we would be protecting trade with China from China, the whole thing is absurd. A clip from the show has been widely circulated and perhaps gives some comedic satisfaction.[7] But it is utterly misinformed. Australian strategic planners already know that it is absurd to protect trade with China from China. That is not the aim of the policy. In the real world, the military build-up is about whether foreign military and intelligence activities can be conducted inside another country's exclusive economic zone (EEZ).

Exclusive economic zones were established as a feature of international law by the United Nations Convention on the Law of the Sea (UNCLOS) in 1982. UNCLOS refers to waters extending up to 200 nautical miles from a country's shores. It gives coastal states the right to regulate economic activities (such as fishing and oil exploration) within their EEZ. The United States has not ratified UNCLOS but says it will act in accordance with its provisions. It established its own EEZ within 200 nautical miles of its coast and recognises the EEZ of other states as well. China has ratified UNCLOS, established its own EEZ and also recognises those of other states.

The United States says further that it has the right to conduct military and intelligence-collection activities within any country's EEZ. It accepts the right of other countries to do this inside its own EEZ; even during the Cold War the United States did not interfere with Soviet ships, bombers or surveillance aircraft that periodically flew close to US airspace. China says it respects freedom of navigation in the South

China Sea but does not respect the right of foreign governments to conduct military and intelligence-collection activities within its EEZ. Admiral Sun Jianguo, deputy chief of China's joint staff, has asked,

> When has freedom of navigation in the South China Sea ever been affected? It has not, whether in the past or now, and in the future there won't be a problem as long as nobody plays tricks ... China consistently opposes so-called military freedom of navigation, which brings with it a military threat and which challenges and disrespects the international law of the sea.[8]

The right to conduct military activities inside another country's EEZ has been at the centre of incidents between US and Chinese ships and aircraft since at least 2001. This issue is separate from the question of territorial disputes in the South China and East China seas. Even if those questions were resolved, China would still oppose 'military freedom of navigation', which the United States insists on. According to an expert from the US Naval War College who testified before Congress, the United States would be forced to conduct military operations from more than 200 miles offshore if China's position on EEZs were to gain greater international acceptance. That would significantly reduce the range of US sensors and missiles, making it much harder to deploy US marines and their equipment in amphibious assaults. Its ability to project naval and air power would face limitations not only in the South China Sea but also in other EEZs such as the Persian Gulf. Its ability to use the world's oceans as a medium of manoeuvre and global power projection would be threatened.[9] Roughly 30 per cent or more of US Navy assets are forward deployed to distant operating areas in the western Pacific, the Indian Ocean–Persian Gulf region, and the waters around Europe. The Navy's largest forward homeporting location is Japan. Its assets are designed to cross broad expanses of ocean and air space, then conduct sustained, large-scale military operations upon arrival in far-off locations.

Article 301 of UNCLOS, entitled 'Peaceful uses of the seas', says that states shall 'refrain from any threat or use of force against the territorial integrity or political independence of any State, or in any other manner inconsistent with the principles of international law embodied in the Charter of the United Nations'. Chinese scholars often begin criticism of US military uses of the EEZ with this provision. The United States knows that Indonesia, the Philippines and India also quietly support the Chinese perspective. In April 2021, the United States carried out a freedom-of-navigation operation 130 nautical miles west of the Lakshadweep Islands, an archipelago of thirty-six tiny but strategically important and ecologically sensitive islands belonging to India. A press release by the commander of the US Seventh Fleet declared that the operation in India's EEZ 'asserted navigational rights and freedoms ... without requesting India's prior consent'.[10] India objected, stating that UNCLOS 'does not authorise other States to carry out in the EEZ and on the continental shelf, military exercises or manoeuvres, in particular those involving the use of weapons or explosives, without the consent of the coastal state'.[11]

Seen in this light, Australia's nuclear-powered submarines are focused not on defending Australia from hostile powers but on supporting the United States in its determination to project power globally. Meanwhile, China has begun to conduct intelligence-gathering and presence operations in other countries' EEZs, including Australia's, justifying its behaviour by saying that it would not do so if Australia adopted its own position on the sovereignty of EEZs. The situation calls for diplomacy and negotiation by all countries, not provocative behaviour. It also calls for mutual strategic empathy: an appreciation of the world as seen through the other side's eyes. Instead what we see is strategic narcissism: planning for other countries' capabilities, not their intentions, but expecting them to be reassured by one's own intentions, regardless of the threat posed by one's capabilities.

AUSFTA–AUKFTA

AUKUS is the military, intelligence and cybersecurity equivalent of the trade agreements Australia has signed with the USA (in 2004) and the UK (in 2021). The three agreements reflect Australia's full-spectrum search for relevance to great power allies in the era of Cold War 2.0. The Australia–United States Free Trade Agreement (AUSFTA) provides important insights into which rules are important in the rules-based international order.[12] It gave a high priority to patents and other intellectual property rights.

Intellectual property rights (IPR) are a high priority for American diplomats. The economist Dani Rodrik points out that today's trade agreements go well beyond traditional border issues like tariffs. They 'seek deep integration among nations'.[13] The first bilateral trade agreement the United States concluded in the postwar period was with Israel, in 1985. It was less than 8,000 words long. Most of it was devoted to border issues. IPR took up a third of a page (and eighty-one words). By contrast, the US–Singapore Free Trade Agreement of 2004 was 70,000 words long and the IPR section alone was longer than the entire US–Israel treaty. Most of it was about behind-the-border topics such as anti-competitive business conduct, electronic commerce, labour, the environment, investment rules, financial services and intellectual property rights.[14] The United States modelled its free trade agreement with Australia on its agreement with Singapore.[15]

AUSFTA expanded the definition of patentable inventions to include 'any new uses or methods of using a known product'. That overturns a long-held view in Australia that 'the discovery of an unknown property in a known material is not patentable, primarily because no manufacture in the sense of a physical thing is disclosed', as the Commissioner of Patents said at a major scientific conference in 1952.[16] There are few good economic reasons to grant a patent merely for a new use of a known substance. As Hazel Moir has argued, a new use of an existing product is just everyday experimentation and is part of normal life. Market mechanisms ought to ensure a good return on investment. After all, the product has already been developed, and the only significant additional cost is marketing.[17]

AUSFTA permits the 'evergreening' of drugs, allowing patents for modifications with a very low level of inventiveness such as new dosages and new methods of using already known compounds. This costs Australian taxpayers—and greatly increases the profits of pharmaceutical companies—while delaying the entry of generic competition into the market.

Although contained within a 'free trade agreement', these are protectionist measures because patents prevent other inventors exploiting their own independently developed inventions. If society is to benefit, then the patent system should allow patents only where the inventions would not have occurred without the patent incentive, and which provide sufficient social benefit to offset the losses from granting the monopoly.

How does the intellectual property rights regime foster Australia's economic dependency and low level of economic complexity? A good example comes from US Embassy cables released by WikiLeaks in 2010. We learn that in 2009 the Labor government rejected a proposal by generic pharmaceuticals companies to produce generic drugs in Australia for export. The embassy reported that the decision occurred 'in light of Australia's international commitments on intellectual property and trade'. It said Australia 'may have preferred to tread lightly on this issue' because its negotiations on intellectual property during AUSFTA 'were particularly difficult'.[18] The decision meant that Australian manufacturers would miss a share of an export market worth US$150 billion over the next six years. Australia might have developed a world-class generic medicines industry had it learned from China's express exclusions from patentability in order to develop a local chemical industry.[19]

The COVID-19 pandemic exemplifies the public policy consequences of the neoliberal project of privatisation, austerity, inequality and the ascendancy of finance capital.[20] For example, in 2022, CSL Limited was a private company with a market capitalisation of $128 billion, making vaccines, antivenins, anticoagulants, pain medicines and other pharmaceutical products. It was founded in 1916 as the Commonwealth Serum Laboratories, which developed antivenins against all major Australian land snakes, developed the first Q fever vaccine and made plasma products. Hundreds of thousands of Australians donated their blood, which is CSL's main input. It was sold for just $292 million in 1994.[21] Australia would be in a different position today had the government not sold the company, or even if it had insisted on retaining 51 per cent equity for the Commonwealth at the very beginning, when share prices were affordable.

The US Embassy in Canberra keeps a close eye on Australia's Pharmaceutical Benefits Scheme (PBS), which subsidises certain medicines. The Australian government, quite understandably, wants these drugs to enter Australia at the lowest possible price—the exact opposite of what foreign drug companies want. Americans sometimes pay up to ten times as much as Australians for identical pharmaceuticals.[22] US Embassy cables released by WikiLeaks show US diplomats reporting that the PBS 'is very popular with the public and medical practitioners, although not with pharmaceutical companies, who complain about PBS's squeezing costs at their expense'. They said that Australia's healthcare system 'appeals to the Australian sense of fairness. Those who can afford to pay more and get more. But there is a basic level of medical care made available for all Australians, regardless of income, insurance, or employment status.' It 'achieves some of the best health outcomes in the OECD despite healthcare spending comprising less than 10 per cent of GDP'.[23]

The status quo also imposes a large cost on Australian consumers. Australia's patent standards have long been set at lower levels than those of its major trading partners. Australia's patents are broader in scope and require the disclosure of less information than overseas. Australia's economic development would be enhanced by eliminating such innovation-stifling protectionism. But it seems to be competing with the United States to award patents to the lowest levels of novelty and inventiveness. Legal scholar Charles Lawson has shown that Australia's High Court places a low threshold on novelty, stipulating only that 'an inventor would be directly led as a matter of course to the invention in the expectation of success'.[24] This means that outcomes from normal experimentation are regarded as inventive. Such a low standard expands the rights and revenues of patent holders but imposes costs on consumers.

In 2021–22, pharmaceutical product imports are expected to total $14.2 billion, nearly three times the amount of exports ($5.1 billion). Furthermore, 'the contribution made by exports is considerably less in net terms, once the high costs of imported ingredients used in local manufacturing processes are taken into account'.[25] Reflecting Australia's lower level of economic development, approximately half the export revenue is from non-prescription pharmaceuticals, including vitamins and dietary supplements, not conventional drugs that are rich in intellectual property. Two decades after joining the World Trade Organization, the Australian public continues to bear the costs of complying with higher intellectual property protectionism. Australia earned only $1.25 billion in royalties for IP exports but paid $4.9 billion in IP imports in 2019–20.[26] This is how the rules-based order works in the real world.

Investment agreements are another demonstration of the imperial order. Their principal or sole aim is to protect foreign investors. They can restrict the ability of states to regulate in the public interest if doing so interferes with certain investor rights—an example of state sovereignty taking a back seat to the interests of private investors. In 2011, the Gillard government introduced the Tobacco Plain Packaging Act to reduce the incidence of smoking, one of the leading causes of preventable deaths. The Act banned logos, symbols and other images on cigarette packs. Philip Morris Asia (PMA) used the Hong Kong–Australia investment treaty to challenge the ban. It launched an action known as Investor–State Dispute Settlement (ISDS), arguing that its cigarettes would 'not be readily distinguishable to the consumer from the products of its competitors; consequently, competition will be based primarily on price'.[27] That was the point of the legislation, after all, but it challenged the company's business model. The litigation resulted in a ruling that the claim was an abuse of process. In April 2011, the Gillard government said it would no longer include ISDS provisions in free trade agreements. The Abbott government reversed this position after the September 2013 election.[28]

Investment agreements with ISDS provisions give corporations rights that no human being possesses. Corporations are not required to go before the local courts in Australia before beginning arbitration, for example. They can directly haul the government before a private arbitration panel. ISDS elevates investor rights above state sovereignty—an imperial arrangement originating in Chile when the Australian Secret Intelligence Service (ASIS) helped the US Central Intelligence Agency overthrow the democratically elected government in 1973.[29] Previously, 'the basic norm governing foreign investment' had been 'national treatment' based on the argument of legal scholar Carlos Calvo that 'foreign investors should not expect special treatment simply because they were foreign. Instead, host states should treat them the same way as domestic investors.'[30] The Chile coup replaced the pro-sovereignty Calvo Doctrine with the investor-rights Washington Consensus.[31]

Investor–State Dispute Settlement may be more expensive than the usual court process because the high costs encourage third-party funding, whereby investors who have no prior interest in the litigation offer to finance it on a contingency basis, taking a percentage of the wins. Many Australian elites are willing participants in this system. 'The entire concept of third-party litigation funding is an Australian invention,' the *Australian*'s legal affairs editor reports. Common law had 'once prevented disinterested parties from financing court cases for a share in the proceeds'.[32] But pro-investor judicial activism cleared the way; in 1996, the Federal Court ruled that commercial litigation funders could raise capital for insolvency practitioners. Ten years later, the High Court held that litigation funders could finance class actions and exercise broad influence over how they are conducted.[33] These judgments transformed the landscape. Unlike courts, ISDS lack standardised rules of procedure. The parties are free to agree on the location, time, confidentiality, witness list and document production. The predictability of outcomes is much lower. No human being enjoys such rights, but corporations—in reality, the elite investors who control them—do. ISDS proceedings are private, not public. Only the final arbitral award is routinely available, and only if the parties agree.[34]

Australia's long-term strategy is to work with like-minded states to replicate investment treaties so widely that they take on the status of customary international law. This, in turn, requires evidence of widespread state practice as well as the belief that such practice is required by international law. If that were to occur, it would have implications for all countries, including those that had not signed investment treaties and those who disputed Western conceptions of customary international law.[35] They would be forced into observing these provisions just to be regarded by other countries as a responsible, law-abiding member of the international community. As yet, of course, customary international law has not been established in investment treaties. They cannot be regarded as codifying norms that would be binding even if there were no treaty. But that is the direction DFAT wants to take us in, and the ASIS–CIA operation to destroy Chilean democracy had the same objective.

AUKUS is thus the military, intelligence and cyber equivalent of Australia's trade and investment agreements with the United States and United Kingdom. Taken as a whole, the agreements uphold the rules-based international order as it actually operates—the rights of private investors take precedence over the sovereignty of (most) states.

4

The China divide

THIS CHAPTER EXAMINES THE challenge of China as an ideological, military and economic challenger to the US-led international order. Chinese competition was responsible for 2.4 million jobs lost in the United States between 1999 and 2011, and in the 2016 Republican primaries Donald Trump 'won 89 of the 100 counties most affected by competition from China'.[1] Australia's Defence Department warned of China's 'active pursuit of greater influence in the Indo-Pacific' and its 'strategic competition' with the United States.[2] Australia will join a chain of US-allied sentinel states whose aim is to encircle China.

What is the Chinese government trying to do?

The government of China operates within an intellectual framework underpinned by a desire for national rejuvenation.

In its view, China's great civilisation was humbled by foreign aggression and its own internal corruption and weakness. The Communist Party sees its victory in 1949 as a double liberation: from external aggression as well as from internal feudalism and obsolete patterns of thought. When Mao Zedong proclaimed the founding of the People's Republic of China in October 1949, the Communist Party of China had 4.5 million members. There were more than three times that number of opium addicts.[3] Today, China is the second largest economy in the world—a status it achieved without resorting to slavery, war or colonialism. Chinese foreign policy is on a mission to restore the country to greatness.

The memory of 'national humiliation' is no rhetorical trope; it is central to Chinese perceptions of strategic realities. As Albert S. Lindemann observed, there have been several appalling chapters in human history: 'All of these were in their own way unique, and all have mysterious, haunting aspects to them, especially to those who identify them as happening to their ancestors.'[4] This mix of optimism and pessimism—what William Callahan calls 'pessoptimism'—informs China's dream of civilisation and its nightmare of humiliation. It is, Callahan writes, 'ever-present in the background as a structure of feeling that guides China's national aesthetic'.[5] Vulnerability, as much as a desire for greatness, guides China's perceptions of strategic realities. In the early decades, China left undeveloped the southern coastal provinces of Guangdong and Fujian, populated by tens of millions of people, because it expected to have to bomb them with its own air force to stave off an invasion by the United States or the regime in Taiwan. In the

1960s, it spent two-thirds of scarce state industrial investment to disperse and conceal its industries from enemy air attack.[6]

Today, China's leader Xi Jinping promotes the 'China Dream' of national rejuvenation. He is described as a large man with the build of an American football player who was sent to the countryside to 'learn from the peasants' after his father lost his post during Mao's purges. Xi was well known to the farmers as a wrestling champion. According to two China experts, he was 'renowned for his ability to carry a shoulder pole of twin 110-pound buckets of wheat for several miles across mountain paths'.[7] US Embassy cables leaked to WikiLeaks describe Xi as an 'exceptionally ambitious, confident and focused' person who 'in early adulthood demonstrated his singleness of purpose by distinguishing himself from his peers'. He 'does not care at all about money and is not corrupt'. He apparently believes that 'rule by a dedicated and committed Communist Party leadership is the key to enduring social stability and national strength'.[8] China's leaders want to strengthen their own legitimacy internally by articulating nationalist goals and counteracting unwelcome ideas, such as Western conceptions of democracy, human rights and freedom of religion.

Elizabeth Economy, senior adviser on China to the US Secretary of Commerce, has suggested that in Xi's vision, China would be the pre-eminent power in Asia while the United States retreated across the Pacific, remaining an Atlantic power but not the sole global superpower.[9] Just as US, European and Japanese companies led infrastructure development in the twentieth century, Chinese companies would compete for leadership in the twenty-first century. Her boss, commerce secretary Gina Raimondo, explained US objectives and strategy to the business press: the United States 'needs to work with Europe to slow China's innovation rate ... We have to work with our European allies to deny China the most advanced technology so that they can't catch up in critical areas like semiconductors.'[10] US policy-makers understand that 'security' means much more than protection from invasion. It is an elastic concept that gives priority to economic interests and to a political order that secures them. They know China does not want to invade or attack the United States. Its threat is its influence on the world via infrastructure ranging from ports, railways and bases to fibre-optic cables, e-payment systems and satellites.

China's most prominent foreign policy project is the Belt and Road Initiative (BRI). The BRI connects China with Central and South Asia, the Middle East and Europe via large infrastructure projects to stimulate trade between China and the Eurasian continent. It encompasses transport, energy infrastructure, telecommunications, smart cities, e-commerce, agriculture, environmental protection, finance, development assistance, civil aviation, accounting and healthcare services. The BRI runs through China's thirteen western provinces, which occupy three-quarters of its land surface but contain only about a quarter of its population. These mountainous or desert provinces contain most of China's mineral resources. Xinjiang, which means 'new frontier', is expected to serve as a BRI hub. The government has no intention of letting Xinjiang's restive indigenous populations get in the way of its ambitions. It subjects its Uyghur, Kazakh, Kyrgyz and other Muslim minorities in the western provinces to a dense network of surveillance systems, checkpoints, interpersonal monitoring and mass imprisonment.

In Xinjiang, the Chinese Communist Party is suspicious of Uyghur ethno-religious identity despite the strong role of identity in the party's own promotion of Chinese nationalism. Party leaders puzzle over why many in the minority populations do not appreciate all that the party has done and why they do not love being part of China, which is ascendant and increasingly wealthy and has invested a lot of money in those regions. Their solution is to assimilate those populations culturally by reducing instruction in their native language and discouraging what Beijing views as strange and threatening religious practices and clothing. The government does not want to destroy the Uyghurs physically but to reduce the significance of their ethnic identities. It would prefer their cultures to be essentially museum pieces—happy minorities in special costumes, but otherwise not that different from the Hakka or Shanghai or Fujian people in China. US Secretary of State Mike Pompeo sought to fire up his evangelical Christian base by emphasising religious rights as the core of human rights and calling China's actions a genocide. Anthropologist Darren Byler's study of China's internment camps shows that many civil rights are suppressed in the process of assimilation.[11]

An underappreciated aspect of the BRI is that it allows China the opportunity to integrate its technical standards into its agreements. Technical standards are the 'specifications or technologies on which other technologies or methods will evolve'.[12] The width of railway gauges, dimensions of shipping containers, shape of electrical sockets and wi-fi standards for wireless networks are examples of previous standards that created lock-in effects and path dependency for future products and technological trajectories. International standards-setting organisations were dominated by experts from the United States, Germany, France, Britain and—to a lesser extent—Japan and Russia. In recent years, China has taken leading roles in the International Organization for Standardisation, the International Telecommunications Union and the International Electrotechnical Commission. It wants to increase the manoeuvrability of its firms abroad. It realises that its failure to act during the telecom 'standards wars' of the 1980s cost it tens of billions of dollars in royalty fees. It also wants to limit critical vulnerabilities introduced by foreign standards in strategic, defence-related sectors.

Standards are a symbol of societal progress and a means of technology transfer. China wants an innovative economy that possesses 'connectivity power' in ports, high-speed rail, regional smart grids and digital 5G-enabled networks through the so-called Digital Silk Roads.[13] The push to climb the technology ladder is threatening to the advanced powers, who object strongly to what they regard as 'forced technology transfer'—a form of intellectual property theft. In 2018, the American Chamber of Commerce in Shanghai said that 21 per cent of 434 respondent member companies had felt pressure to transfer technology in exchange for market access.[14] In high-tech industries, 44 per cent of aerospace and 41 per cent of chemical companies faced 'notable' pressure to transfer technology. China replied by saying that it did not want to forever remain an assembly area for Western tech companies; they came to China to take advantage of cheap labour, and China should benefit too. Matt Sheehan, a specialist on the US–China technology relationship, writes that the 'largest impact' of China's scientific and commercial ties to leading US companies, universities, and labs 'came not from stealing, but instead from learning. Exposure to world-class innovative processes gave China the intellectual fodder—the ideas, best practices, and operating models—that it needed to ignite its nascent tech ecosystem.'[15]

The United States has responded by cutting off supplies of semiconductors to leading Chinese firms. The move is expected to weaken their international competitiveness because China relies heavily on semiconductor imports. It spends more on imported silicon than it does on oil.[16] Its ability to manufacture advanced logic chips at scale lags well behind that of the leading US firms. Most of its semiconductor foundry companies are at least one and a half generations behind. It has no tier-one semiconductor equipment firms, defined as direct suppliers to original equipment manufacturers (OEMs). It has just one tier-two semiconductor equipment company, defined as a key supplier to a tier-one supplier.[17] Chinese companies depend on software and equipment from US-based corporations such as Cadence, Synopsys, Applied Materials and Lam Research. The United States is determined to stop China narrowing the gap in technological prowess.

The new 'digital iron curtain' dividing the world into US and Chinese technological zones runs through Australia, which has banned Huawei from supplying equipment to Australia's 5G network. The technical nature of 5G systems makes it almost impossible to conduct timely security investigations at the time of purchase; likewise the ability to prevent malicious functionality from entering through software updates.

These features, combined with the expected central role 5G will play in Western societies, mean that screening or similar control mechanisms cannot address security concerns involving espionage and sabotage.[18] Information leaked by Edward Snowden shows that the US National Security Agency has undertaken what it calls 'supply chain enabling, exploitation, or intervention operations', including 'hardware implant enabling, exploitation or operations'.[19] It intercepts shipments of computer network devices such as servers and routers, unseals them and instals beacon implants directly into these devices. It then repackages them and sends them along to the original destination. The NSA thus gains controlled backdoors in the 'internet backbone', providing potential access to an entire country's core communication infrastructure. Huawei-supplied infrastructure would interfere with the United States' ability to keep spying at this industrial-level scale—and would potentially allow China to do so as well.

China is said to engage in cyber-espionage to help it climb the technology ladder. This is not surprising; as Doron Ben-Atar points out in his study of industrial innovation, 'Every major European state engaged in technology piracy and industrial espionage in the eighteenth century.'[20] The United States could not afford to act any differently, and did not. Stealing intellectual property was a linchpin of its manufacturing strategy, and one reason why it had an industrial revolution in the first place. In the late eighteenth century, Britain had criminalised the export of textile machinery and knowhow. The United States stole the knowhow by offering bounties to attract immigrants like Samuel Slater, who had a detailed knowledge of textile machinery. With US financial backing, he constructed versions of British spinning and carding machinery and established the first successful cotton mill in the United States in 1793. Two decades later, there were another 140 mills in a 30-mile radius, and the US textile industry was launched. As Ben-Atar writes, 'Political self-determination, economic independence, and technology piracy seemed to go hand in hand.'[21]

Piracy continued into the twentieth century, when Germany was the leading industrial power in advanced chemical processes, especially in dyes and nitrates. But the United States took over German patents and technology after World War I and made them available to US industry, 'paving the way for a formidable rise in US domestic production that substituted for the German imports. A new patent-intensive, science-based American industry emerged.'[22] The Versailles Treaty's expropriation mechanisms gave the Allies far-reaching confiscatory powers over German property, rights and interests around the world. IG Farben and other German firms were forced to share their patents. Major US chemical companies such as Du Pont rose to pre-eminence as a result. They were further helped by policies that sheltered the infant US chemical industry that had emerged during World War I. Industrial development and economic growth since then have been heavily reliant on the plastics industry: neoprene, polystyrene, nylon, Teflon, polyester, Kevlar and more. China's attitude to intellectual property in the twenty-first century is no doubt informed by its awareness of historical realities.

Although China recognises that it is a major power, it also sees itself as first among a group of large developing countries. This stance means that it has common interests with developing states on many issues. It has called for a more democratic international order; it works with like-minded countries to gain a greater say in how international economic and political institutions are structured and administered. Even India, its South Asian rival, aligns its votes in the UN General Assembly more with Beijing than with Washington. China says its relationships with the developing world must go beyond profits to include a 'sense of justice'—a sentiment that many developing countries find attractive. It is setting up a network of technical training colleges around the world to train foreign students in industrial sensors, control and robotics technologies, machinery equipment manufacturing and high-speed rail technologies. Known as the Luban Workshops after Lu Ban, a mythical figure revered as an inventor, the students will be trained in Chinese technology with Chinese standards as part of a push to globalise Chinese technology and tighten the economic linkages between China and the Global South. According to foreign policy scholars Niva Yau and Dirk van der Kley, 'the Chinese government has been willing to listen to host countries involved in the Belt and Road Initiative' and help them transfer industrial skills to their own economies and develop their own societies, within the Chinese orbit and using Chinese technology.[23]

What do the Chinese people think about their one-party state?

The Harvard Ash Center for Democratic Governance and Innovation designed the longest-running independent effort to track Chinese citizens' sentiments about all four levels of government (town, county, province, central government). It collected data in eight separate waves between 2003 and 2016, recording the face-to-face interview responses of more than 31,000 individuals in both urban and rural settings. It found a 'near-universal increase in Chinese citizens' average satisfaction toward all four levels of government'. Marginalised groups in poorer, inland regions were more likely to be satisfied. The study concluded that 'there was no real sign of burgeoning discontent among China's main demographic groups, casting doubt on the idea that the country was facing a crisis of political legitimacy'.[24]

When Xi Jinping became president in March 2013, he launched the biggest anti-corruption campaign in China's history, arresting more than 120 high-level party leaders and more than 100,000 lower-level government officials. The *Financial Times* reports that the campaign was 'unparalleled in its scale and longevity, ensnaring about two million officials over 10 years'. Some suspects have fled overseas, with Australia, New Zealand, Canada and the United States being 'the most popular destinations for China's most-wanted fugitives ... Their escapes are normally well-planned, with large amounts of capital concealed, transferred or laundered over many years.'[25] More than 70 per cent of respondents in the Ash Center study approved of Xi's anti-corruption efforts in 2016. And, while only 35 per cent viewed Chinese government officials as generally 'clean' in 2011, 65 per cent did in 2016.

The Chinese public's concern about the environment continues to increase, with good reason: they have seen their vulnerability to H5N1 avian flu, H1N1 swine flu and now SARS-CoV-2. A Ministry of Environmental Protection study found that nearly two-thirds of underground water and a third of surface water was 'unsuitable for human contact', contaminated by fertiliser run-offs, heavy metals and untreated sewage.[26] Air pollution causes more than one million premature Chinese deaths a year, and less than 1 per cent of the urban population breathes air considered safe by European Union standards. Massive canal systems have been built to transfer water from the southern rivers to the densely populated North China Plain. Global warming will cause northern aquifers to dry up in two decades, at the same time as the melting Tibetan glaciers will reduce the flow of water in the southern rivers. Soil contamination, deforestation, desertification and habitat loss round out the picture. Environmental issues are the biggest motivator of citizen complaints and mass protests. Citizens expect the government to act. In 2016, 75 per cent of the population believed that climate change is real and caused by human behaviour, and nearly 70 per cent supported enacting a nation-wide emissions tax—higher than in Australia (62 per cent in 2019) or the United States (44 per cent in 2018).[27]

The government enjoys a high level of popular support for many reasons. One is the steady rise in living standards. The central government promotes local officials who have shown competence in growing the economy, maintaining population growth within planning targets, managing social protests, and other managerial tasks. The government delegates considerable authority to the local party organisation, which delivers results in large, complex jurisdictions. Five of China's thirty-three province-level units have populations larger than 80 million—the population of the largest European country,

Germany. This kind of 'responsive authoritarianism' is poorly understood in Australia.[28] The party's 90 million members and 4 million grassroots party organisations helped shape China's rapid containment of the coronavirus pandemic. Urban civil organisations (*juweihui*) organised mutual safety and mutual aid in their neighbourhoods. In Wuhan, members of these neighbourhood committees went door-to-door to check temperatures and deliver food and medical supplies.[29] Lacking a similar organisation that supports social resilience, Australia had to deploy its military and emergency services and hire private contractors.

A second reason for popular support is China's 'never again' attitude to Western imperialism.[30] Unlike in neighbouring India, postwar Chinese leaders were not in thrall to Anglophilia. The education system ensures that all Chinese understand the consequences of weakness in the face of Western power. A third reason is the absence of independent journalism. China has an authoritarian political system. Whoever challenges it takes a risk. Censorship is both overt and covert. Another important reason is the success of the Central Propaganda Department. Anne-Marie Brady's scholarly study of this high-level party office shows that Noam Chomsky's analysis of the American media system is 'extremely influential among propaganda and mass communication theorists in China'.[31] Chinese propagandists have studied Chomsky's work with Edward Herman on 'manufacturing consent' and applied it to their own system. They encourage 'diversity and contention within a permitted range of subjects' in order to 'render invisible the subjects forbidden by the regime and placed outside the perimeter'. Accordingly, 'Chinese readers feel they are living in an environment of freedom' and have 'no way to break into the monopoly circle that decides on the fundamental issues that confront their society'. There is a 'social contract that allows the children to have their sly fun so long as the grown-ups run the house'. The 'end result of this sophisticated cultural programming differs little from the mass media in the West, where just as in China nothing important is discussed'.[32]

The COVID-19 pandemic illustrates the effect of this propaganda system. The Communist Party turned the pandemic into a political asset by censoring criticism of its early missteps and highlighting its later success in sharply reducing infections. There was no apology or compensation for the damage caused worldwide, only triumphant rhetoric and claims of selfless altruism. A good analogy to this nationalist mythologising may be found in Eric Williams' remark that 'British historians write almost as if Britain had introduced Negro slavery solely for the satisfaction of abolishing it'.[33] Internationally, however, views of China have grown more negative across fourteen advanced economies, and unfavourable opinion soared in 2020. Negative views of China increased most in Australia, where 81 per cent of people view it unfavourably, an increase of 24 percentage points since the previous year.[34]

If China's party state were replaced by a multiparty democracy, it would continue its military modernisation. It would continue to assert its claims in the East and South China seas, where it has increased its maritime patrols and built large artificial islands on existing reefs and rocks in disputed waters also claimed by such countries as the Philippines and Vietnam. It has backed these up by combining four of its five maritime agencies into a vast coast guard. It has also developed a 'counter-intervention' strategy involving asymmetrical weaponry to blunt the United States' military advantages. China now possesses an arsenal of high-speed ballistic missiles, known to Western military planners as 'anti-access/area denial' (A2/AD), designed to strike moving ships. These so-called carrier killers can threaten the most powerful vessels in the US fleet at a considerable distance from China's coast.[35]

China's priority is not to invade or occupy areas of the Asia Pacific (with the notable exception of Taiwan) but rather to raise the cost of hostile US action. Like many countries, China works with governments of all types, including one-party or authoritarian regimes, to advance its economic and diplomatic interests but makes no attempt to impose a distinctly Chinese domestic system on others. It also lacks an alliance of the size and structure of NATO. In the wake of the Ukraine crisis, Russia is likely to drift further into China's orbit, supplying raw materials while China incorporates more and more of the world into the Belt and Road Initiative.

China's intentions towards Taiwan

To understand what drives China's policy on Taiwan, we need some insight into its leaders' self-understanding. In particular, what do they see as their national territory? From their point of view, it includes Taiwan. They claim that Taiwan is their territory and point to a version of history to support their claim. Like most claims of this nature, it blends modern and pre-modern concepts of sovereignty. China is not alone; India and Pakistan, for example, both claim Kashmir as part of their national territory and neither accepts an independent Kashmiri state. A consistent thread runs through China's statements about Taiwan. The five key leaders since 1949—Mao Zedong, Deng Xiaoping, Jiang Zemin, Hu Jintao and Xi Jinping—have had very different personalities, interests and outlooks, but have all insisted that Taiwan is an integral part of China. The Australian government has sharply escalated its internal preparations in anticipation of a potential conflict there, and Australia might well be asked to contribute its submarines, air warfare destroyers, maritime surveillance aircraft, air-to-air refuellers, Super Hornet fighters and some Army elements as part of a US-led force.[36]

Taiwan is not just a key unresolved issue from the past; today its multiparty democracy also represents an ideological challenge to China's party-state political system, as did the democracy movement in Hong Kong. It is valuable for strategic and economic reasons as well. Control over Taiwan would solve China's geographic problem by giving it unrestricted access to the Pacific Ocean. Naval bases on Taiwan's east coast would allow China's submarine fleet to conduct patrols in the deep waters of the Pacific. These bases would be only 180 kilometres away from the disputed Senkaku Islands (administered by Japan but claimed by China, which calls them the Diaoyu Islands). From there, Chinese forces would be able to deter Japanese and US forces on Okinawa, perhaps pressuring Japan to evict US forces from Okinawa and terminate the 1960 Treaty of Mutual Cooperation and Security between the United States and Japan.

Taiwan is also the site of one of the linchpins of the global economy: Taiwan Semiconductor Manufacturing Company

(TSMC), the world's most advanced semiconductor factory. It is building a plant to make transistors—the key building block in computer chips—just three nanometres in size, the length your fingernail grows in three seconds. The smaller the transistors on a chip, the lower the energy consumption and the higher the speed. The new chips will be up to 70 per cent faster than the most advanced in production now. The plant is the size of twenty-two football fields and is considered the 'centre of the universe' in the world of semiconductors.[37] It is also key to high-end weapons production, supplying processors to supercomputers that model missile trajectories, as well as for the missiles themselves. Its value will only increase in an era of unmanned combat systems such as combat drones. Under US pressure, TSMC has halted sales to Chinese supercomputer maker Phytium, and is building a US$12 billion plant in Arizona.

Lonnie Henley, an East Asia expert with forty years of experience in US intelligence, testified before Congress that China began planning in earnest for a potential conflict with the United States over Taiwan after the May 1999 bombing of the Chinese embassy in Belgrade. He said, 'From China's perspective, the bombing and the larger Kosovo conflict were a major geostrategic event: a US-led coalition acting without UN authorization, invading a sovereign state and carving off a province of that state to become independent just because Americans thought it should be.' Henley spoke of the 'rampant unilateralism and disregard of international norms, plus the specifically anti-China focus of the embassy bombing (which no Chinese I have ever spoken to believes was a mistake)'. According to Henley, 'a long-term air, maritime, and information blockade of Taiwan' could be 'the main effort, eschewing an attempted landing altogether, or it could be part of a larger invasion campaign'. But even if the landing failed, China 'could continue the blockade indefinitely and neither US nor Taiwan forces would have much ability to overcome it'.[38]

Australia's participation

What would Australia do if the United States went to war against China? Such a question has been discussed candidly behind closed doors. In 2006, opposition leader Kim Beazley told the US ambassador that 'Australia would have absolutely no alternative but to line up militarily beside the US. Otherwise the alliance would be effectively dead and buried, something that Australia could never afford to see happen.'[39] Beazley's candour is important because he did not expect WikiLeaks to publish his remarks less than five years later. A few days later, US Embassy staff met his principal political adviser, Jim Chalmers, whom the embassy wanted to 'protect' as an interlocutor.[40] Chalmers is now a leading figure in Australian politics. He has not yet spoken publicly on whether 'Australia would have absolutely no alternative but to line up militarily beside the US', but former defence minister Peter Dutton already declared that 'it would be inconceivable that we wouldn't support the US in an action if the US chose to take that action ... Maybe there are circumstances where we wouldn't take up that option. I can't conceive of those circumstances.'[41]

What would such a conflict look like? In 2016, the RAND Corporation warned that a war between the United States and

China 'could be intense, last a year or more, have no winner, and inflict huge losses and costs on both sides'. Both sides 'have an incentive to strike enemy forces before being struck by them'. While in 2016 Chinese losses would greatly exceed US losses, 'by 2025, that gap could be much smaller'.[42] Australian analyst Crispin Rovere notes that RAND underestimates the likelihood of a war on the Korean Peninsula:

> The correct military decision for China would be to place enough pressure on the South to force America to commit large-scale forces to the defence, without overwhelming it immediately and presenting the US with a fait accompli. Once committed, the US would be in a diabolical military situation. Hundreds of thousands of US land forces would be engaged against an enormous number of enemy combatants, supported by vulnerable supply lines in highly contested waters near the Chinese mainland. Indeed, it is perfectly likely a war that started in the Spratlys could be lost by the US at Busan.[43]

Australia's war planners no doubt recognise that the Australian Army could be asked to join the US in high-intensity conflict on the Korean Peninsula.

The RAND study mentions Australia just twice, and assumes its support for the United States. Missing from its strategic analysis of numbers and types of weapons is the social fracture that Australia would suffer. As casualties mounted, there would be calls from the political fringes for Chinese Australians to be interned in camps. There would also be massive economic disruption to trade in the western Pacific, since 95 per cent of Chinese trade is seaborne. The last time Australians were killed by enemy air power was in Salamaua in Papua New Guinea in 1943. The last time Australia was involved in a high-intensity war was also on the Korean Peninsula, almost seventy years ago. There was little substantial debate, let alone disagreement, about the nature, length, objectives and strategy of the twenty-year-long presence in Afghanistan. China is not the Taliban, which lacked even the most basic form of air power. A clash with China could be a turning point in Australian history.

The south-west Pacific

In April 2022, news emerged that China and Solomon Islands had entered into an agreement involving ship visits, logistical replenishment and other related activities. The opposition said it was the 'worst failure of Australian foreign policy in the Pacific since the end of World War II'.[44] With less hyperbole, independent Senator Rex Patrick called it 'Australia's worst intelligence failure' in more than two decades and said that Australia's high commissioner, other senior diplomatic staff, Australian Defence Force representatives, the Australian Secret Intelligence Service and the Australian Signals Directorate 'should all face very searching questions about their performance in what appears to be an intelligence failure of major proportions'.[45] Some journalists reported claims that Australia's intelligence agencies were not caught napping.[46]

There is a way to deal with this question, particularly since the opposition claimed to be outraged too. The government, with bipartisan support, could declassify the intelligence it received by sanitising it to conceal the specific means by which it was obtained. Sanitisation preserves the agencies' ability to continue to obtain intelligence on the target. For example, the Office of National Assessments and the Defence Intelligence Organisation produce intelligence assessments that draw on communications intelligence (the preserve of the Australian Signals Directorate) and human intelligence (the preserve of the Australian Secret Intelligence Service). The assessments are analytical reports whose conclusions can be published without disclosing the details of technical and human sources. That would be a simple way to examine whether the intelligence agencies gave advance warning—and, if so, of what kind—without enabling foreign governments and other hostile elements to take adequate countermeasures against Australia.

The United States, which takes oversight of intelligence agencies seriously, held an inquiry after its intelligence community failed to provide warning of India's nuclear tests in 1998. The director of central intelligence appointed a panel of outside experts, chaired by Admiral David Jeremiah, a former vice-chairman of the Joint Chiefs of Staff. The report remains classified, but Admiral Jeremiah provided an unclassified description of his group's findings. He talked about the problems in collecting information about the Indian program, as well as about analysts who refused to believe that the government would carry through on its promise to conduct nuclear tests, and discussed his recommendations. He also responded to questions regarding the seriousness of the intelligence failure, the role of Indian security measures in preventing US detection of test plans, and whether with warning of India's plans the US government could have taken diplomatic action to prevent the tests. The United States also released an unclassified list with specific recommendations for improvement.[47] Australia could do something similar if it chooses.

Solomon Islands has considerable challenges. It ranked 151st in the 2020 Human Development Report, placing it in the Low Human Development category. It is a youthful country in which seven out of ten people are younger than 30 years of age. The danger of large numbers of young people who lack income-generating activities or other outlets for their energy and ambition is well known. The neoliberal framework within which Australia has engaged with the region has not delivered optimal social outcomes. Why would it, given its track record? In this context, development along the Chinese infrastructure-based model might offer improvements in the standard of living. And that could send a message to Australia's traditional vassals in the region—who are sometimes called 'our Pacific family'. If they see material improvements in the lives of Solomon Islanders, they would not necessarily fear closer integration with the Chinese economy.

Chinese aid is attractive to Solomon Islands because it largely stays in Solomon Islands; Australian aid does not. During the Australian-led Regional Assistance Mission to Solomon Islands (RAMSI), about half the aid went towards the salaries of the Australian Federal Police. Some of the remainder went to paying advisers to the public service, employing magistrates and running the country's prison system. This is a form of 'boomerang aid' that simply returns to Australia, since most of the foreign consultants or in-line appointees were Australian anyway. As Aid/Watch, the aid monitoring group put it, Australia was 'the largest direct recipient of its own aid funding'.[48]

The Chinese government behaves respectfully towards these much smaller countries, who in turn are drawn to China's promise of economic development rather than 'boomerang aid'. They recognise that China is no alien trespasser but has long been part of the western Pacific. Chinese navigation texts referred to the island of Timor centuries ago; in the fourteenth century, a Chinese merchant wrote that its 'mountains have no trees other than sandalwood in great abundance' and that 'silver and iron bowls, Western silk cloth and coloured kerchiefs are traded'.[49] The south-west Pacific will be the scene of intensifying competition in the years ahead.

Mutual strategic empathy means understanding that China does not take a benign view of its encirclement by the US Indo-Pacific Command, which doubled its spending in fiscal year 2022, in part to develop 'a network of precision-strike missiles along the so-called first island chain'.[50] China therefore seeks to limit US and Australian interference with its operations against Taiwan, rather than to conquer Australia. As Christopher Joye puts it, 'China's strategic goal is to prevent Australia from getting involved in the potential conflict over the future of Taiwan's democracy, and, more specifically, neutralising Australian and US signals intelligence and surveillance assets that would be crucial to this campaign.'[51]

In 2013, the Philippines brought a legal case against China before an international panel. It concerned activities and claims in the South China Sea. The panel ruled against China in 2016, finding that there was no evidence that China had exercised exclusive control historically over that body of water. China ignored the panel and disregarded its verdict. Amid calls for China to respect the outcome, a few points should be noted. International law expert Professor Natalie Klein points out that Japan immediately said that the judgment 'had not set a precedent but was only binding as between the Philippines and China, and did not apply to Okinotorishima', an island roughly halfway between Taiwan and Guam that is claimed by Japan, Korea, China and Taiwan. Japan also asserts rights over the continental shelf and exclusive economic zones off the disputed Senkaku (Diaoyu) and Takeshima (Dokdo) islands, as well as from Minamitori-shima in the Pacific, but they arguably 'would not meet the requirements of sustaining human habitation or an economic life of their own' as defined in the 2016 judgment.[52]

Likewise, the judgment calls into question the United States' own claims to extended maritime zones around Johnston Atoll, which lies in the North Pacific Ocean, approximately 1400 km south-west of Hawaii, and many of the outlying features in the Aleutians or north-west Hawaiian Islands, which might not count as 'islands' under the tribunal's judgment. Related questions arise about Australia's claims off both the Heard and McDonald Islands, located approximately 4,000 km south-west of Western Australia. According to the Australian Antarctic Division, 'Since the first landing on Heard Island in 1855, there have been only approximately 240 shore-based visits to the island, and only two landings on McDonald Island (in 1971 and 1980).'[53] Australia also relies on small and uninhabited features to claim extended jurisdiction in maritime boundary delimitations with France in relation to New Caledonia. This is not the same as permanent settlement or exclusive historical control.

If these matters are not presented to the Australian public in a meaningful way, people cannot be blamed for thinking that China is the world's major rogue state hell-bent on disregarding international law. In chapter 5 we turn to the question of public opinion.

5

Expertise, secrecy and ideology

They who have put out the people's eyes reproach them of their blindness.

John Milton, 1642

IN JUNE 2021, CHIEF of the Defence Force General Angus Campbell appeared before parliament to take stock of Australia's longest war, the twenty-year mission in Afghanistan. He assured parliament that the Australian Defence Force had 'helped to improve the security of millions of Afghans'. It had helped 'develop the Afghan national defence and security forces and train and advise many thousands of Afghan officers and soldiers'. He confidently dismissed claims that the Taliban would overrun Afghanistan once NATO and its allies left. 'This is very much going to be a negotiated settlement,' he said. 'I do not think that the situation is at all assured in terms of the Taliban's claimed ascendance—or that they seek to claim. I think this is very much going to be a negotiated settlement.'[1] Peter Jennings, a prominent strategic affairs commentator and head of the Australian Strategic Policy Institute, praised General Campbell's comments, saying that 'the only person who thinks there is no chance of military victory in Afghanistan is Joe Biden', who had ordered the withdrawal of US forces.[2]

Within two months, the Afghanistan government's forces had lost control of the entire rural countryside. The Taliban then captured the capital, Kabul, and all thirty-three provincial capitals in less than two weeks. The president of Afghanistan fled the country in a helicopter, reportedly taking US$150 million in cash with him as he headed for the United Arab Emirates.[3] General Campbell admitted that he was 'surprised by the speed of the Taliban's takeover' but said he 'didn't know of anyone who predicted how quickly the collapse would occur "other than in the glory of 20:20 hindsight"'.[4] In fact, the collapse of the US-backed Afghan army in 2021 resembled the US-backed Iraqi army's collapse in 2014, when 30,000 Iraqi soldiers in Mosul fled before a tiny force of perhaps 800 Islamic State militants. In both cases, the insurgents captured intact large quantities of US military hardware and weapons. In both cases, the client regimes were racked by corruption and a crisis of legitimacy. Lessons could have been learnt because there were important similarities.

Why did Australia's commentators, military chief and intelligence agencies get it so badly wrong? It was not because of technical inferiority; the United States and Australia could record and save every telephone call in that country. An intelligence collection program called MYSTIC allowed them to scrape Afghanistan's mobile networks for 'metadata': information about the time, location, source and destination of calls. Another program called SOMALGET allowed them to vacuum up and store the contents of every conversation in the country, then rewind and replay them up to thirty days in the past, even between individuals who had not been specifically targeted for surveillance.[5] It certainly was not because of insufficient time in Afghanistan; they had twenty years of in-depth exposure to Afghanistan's society and its leaders. They had virtually unlimited amounts of money; the United States spent more on Afghanistan than it did on the Marshall Plan to reconstruct Europe after World War II.[6] In its twenty years there, it spent more than US$2 trillion on the war in Afghanistan, or US$300 million a day, every day, for two decades.[7] The Australian government has not yet published the full costs of its own twenty-year presence, but estimates are reported to range from A$7.8 billion to $13.6 billion.[8]

Why the Australian intelligence community apparently performed so poorly ought to be the subject of a no-holds-barred inquiry—one that seeks to discover the truth rather than conceal it. But a bipartisan consensus protects the system from genuine inquiry. The ship of state has sailed on, this time to the Taiwan Strait. Prominent national security experts on Afghanistan have pivoted smoothly to becoming commentators on China and its intentions. Everyone is polite enough not to mention that it took twenty years, trillions of dollars, six

Australian prime ministers and four US presidents to replace the Taliban ... with the Taliban.

Expertise

What counts as expertise in international relations, foreign affairs, national security or politics more generally? One answer was given by US strategist Henry Kissinger: an expert is someone skilled in 'elaborating and defining' the consensus of the powerful: 'those who have a vested interest in commonly held opinions'. This is the constituency that matters. 'Elaborating and defining its consensus at a high level has, after all, made him an expert.'[9] In this sense, commentators who defended the twenty-year war in Afghanistan were experts; they elaborated and defined the consensus of the powerful. There were debates and disagreements among these commentators, to be sure—over narrow tactical issues within a shared framework of agreement. There was a broad consensus that Australian forces should be in Iraq and Afghanistan along with US forces. The debate was over what kinds of forces Australia should provide and how to fight the war—tactics, not fundamentals.

There is another test of expertise, however: consequences. What were the reasonably foreseeable consequences of the policy, and did they occur? Recent examples are illuminating. The foreseeable consequences of the invasion of Iraq were, as Britain's Joint Intelligence Committee warned, a sharp increase in the threat of terrorism. The committee's assessment of 10 February 2003 said, 'The threat from Al-Qaida will increase at the onset of any military action against Iraq.' It said the 'worldwide threat from other Islamist terrorist groups and individuals will increase significantly'.[10] The British government declassified this assessment during an inquiry into the war. Australia has not held such an inquiry and has not declassified its assessments. But the obvious deduction is that the Australian government acted despite knowing that its actions would increase the threat to the Australian public. The invasion of Iraq reveals the reality behind the Foreign Policy White Paper's claim that 'the security of the Australian nation' is 'the core of foreign and trade policy'. It shows that security is not directly understood as the safety of the Australian public but as enhancing Australia's relevance to the United States' global primacy. That in turn is understood as maintaining Australia's current privileged position in the world.

An enabling objective—one that makes this first-order objective possible—is the shaping of Australian public opinion. A secret Australian Army study of the Iraq war said that one of the key objectives was to maintain 'Australian public support for the role of the ADF in actively supporting global security'.[11] 'Global security' is a euphemism for 'US military operations' since whatever the United States does supports 'global security'—a hallmark of the 'rules-based international order'. It enjoys the support of the 'international community'—meaning the global superpower and whoever agrees with it. The Australian Army study said that Australia's 'true strategic intent' was 'to improve its relations with the United States' because 'the conflict's centre of gravity was the opinion of policy-makers in Washington. Favourably influencing this opinion was Australia's principal policy goal.'[12] That is not what most people remember about the Howard government's pre-war rhetoric.

The Howard government claimed that it was motivated by the sanctity of UN Security Council Resolutions and the spread of weapons of mass destruction and, later, the rebuilding of the Iraqi nation. The Army's secret study said that all this was only 'mandatory rhetoric'.[13] It said, 'The true centre of gravity from Canberra's perspective was to not jeopardise the Washington alliance.'[14] The public could not hold the government to account because both sides of politics avoided debating that central objective. That objective—the overriding importance of US priorities—is not a complicated concept beyond the comprehension of the average person. No specialised training is needed to understand it. But doctrinal constraints make it difficult to admit that the United States is an imperial power and the rules-based international order is a US-led imperial order.

The same test of expertise can be applied to the twenty-year war in Afghanistan. In 1996, al-Qaeda 'was a shell of an organization, reduced to some thirty members', according to the Australian Federal Police's former senior counterterrorism intelligence analyst. Before Australian troops entered Afghanistan in October 2001, al-Qaeda's membership 'included a core of just under 200 people, a 122-person martyrdom brigade, and several dozen foot soldiers'.[15] Twenty years later, the threat of Islamist terror has expanded from a small corner of Afghanistan to a much wider area of the globe. The invasion of Iraq, the destruction of Libya and the continuing mayhem caused by drone warfare in the Middle East and North Africa—supported through the intelligence facilities at

Pine Gap—have resulted in a massive expansion of terrorist activity. The policies have therefore harmed national security (understood in its non-ideological sense) while enhancing state power. If expertise is measured by consequences, especially for the safety of the Australian public or the wider world, then the dismal track record speaks for itself.

These events show that the organising principle of Australian foreign policy is to stay on the winning side of the global confrontation between developed and developing countries, between North and South, between imperialism and anti-colonialism. In this subimperial sense, the wars in Iraq and Afghanistan were successful; the Australian flag flew alongside the Star-Spangled Banner, demonstrating Australia's contribution to the US effort. Military activities in Afghanistan and Iraq were less important than having senior US figures visit the Australian area of operations. Australia's long presence in Afghanistan was tied to US domestic politics rather than the military situation on the ground in Afghanistan. Specifically, it was tied to the US election cycle: after the Taliban's comeback in 2008, the Obama administration did not want to be attacked in congressional or presidential elections for being unable to defeat the Taliban. The election of President Trump, with his unconventional approach, finally made it possible for his successor President Biden to withdraw without being attacked for losing the war.

Prime Minister Morrison announced that Australian troops would be withdrawn less than twenty-four hours after the United States announced its own withdrawal first. The timing shows the overriding importance of US priorities for Australia's mission in Afghanistan: its length, its objectives and its futility. A good illustration of this fact is the case of Mr Hekmatullah, the Afghan army sergeant who murdered three Australian soldiers in August 2012. Instead of receiving the death penalty, he joined the Taliban delegation in Qatar. The United States did not block his early release from prison. Hugh Poate, father of one of the murdered Australian soldiers, said the US practice of 'pandering to the wishes of a terrorist group' rather than respecting 'the sacrifice of soldiers and families of its longstanding ally' was 'a damning indictment of the Australian–American "alliance"'.[16]

The policies have been carried out in the knowledge that they increase the terrorist threat, but Australian foreign policy is a matter of priorities. Showing relevance to the United States is a higher priority, and counterterrorism is subordinate to it. That means giving greater powers of surveillance to the intelligence and security agencies, not to altering the policies that make terrorist threats likely in the first place. If you stick to those doctrinal limitations, you qualify as an expert. In government, neither side of politics has ordered an inquiry into the Iraq war, and the director-general of the Australian Security Intelligence Organisation is not pressed on the most obvious question when he appears before parliament: do Australia's military expeditions raise or lower the threat to domestic security? If you fear the answer, better not ask the question. As George Orwell wrote, certain things go unmentioned because of

> a general tacit agreement that 'it wouldn't do' to mention that particular fact … At any given moment there is an orthodoxy, a body of ideas which it is assumed that all

> right-thinking people will accept without question. It is not exactly forbidden to say this, that or the other but it is 'not done' to say it ... Anyone who challenges the prevailing orthodoxy finds himself silenced with surprising effectiveness.[17]

Secrecy

The secrecy surrounding Australian foreign and defence policy protects planners from the public that elected them. The war in Afghanistan offers ample evidence. The United States and Australia carried out an assassination campaign against the tactical leadership of the insurgency. Known as the Joint Priority Effects List (JPEL), it is an intelligence-driven assassination program enabled by drones and special forces. The dynamic involves assassinating insurgents without dealing with the root causes of the insurgency. The dead leader would typically be replaced quickly by a younger, more competent and more vicious one. Some Australian forces participated in this assassination campaign, which was known by various euphemisms. By 2009, US intelligence reports indicated that most insurgents in Afghanistan were not religiously motivated Taliban, let alone al-Qaeda, but a 'new generation of tribal fighters' who had opposed the Taliban during the 1990s. They were mostly ethnic Pashtuns who were 'deeply connected by family and social ties' to their tribal areas and opposed the United States 'because it is an occupying power'.[18]

The JPEL-based assassination program was no secret to the Taliban, nor to the population of Afghanistan, some of whom were killed or maimed while merely attending weddings or tending their farms. Nor was it a secret to the intelligence services of neighbouring states like Russia, China, Iran and Pakistan. But it *was* a secret to the Australian public, who had no way to hold the government to account. Instead, the Australian Defence Force gave prominence to Sarbi, a black Labrador explosives detection dog who became separated from her handler, presumed dead, to be found again a year later. For the next year and a half, the ADF issued nine press releases about what Kevin Foster called her 'quasi-biblical journey from exile and suffering in the wilderness to the warm embrace of home and family'.[19] One can hardly blame Australians for lacking expertise when they are deliberately kept in the dark.

Policy-makers usually claim they have a unique ability to judge what constitutes harm to national security. In relation to AUKUS, foreign minister Marise Payne said: '[N]obody who is not part of those discussions and is not part of the decision-making process can ever know—and frankly nor should they know—the detail and the depth of the considerations that governments go into. These have to be done in a confidential way.'[20] But secrecy in these circumstances does not protect the Australian public. Rather, it protects the security establishment from knowledge of its actions by the Australian public. It allows planners to uphold the US-led imperial order under the guise of Australia's national interest. It insulates the real aims of policy from robust, evidence-based debate. This is not national security in any meaningful sense.

For all the mystique and secrecy, practitioners have not demonstrated that they possess some special body of technical knowledge that renders them uniquely qualified to determine what constitutes a legitimate reason for secrecy. Concepts in national security, foreign affairs and the social sciences more generally are accessible to the average human being, who has what Descartes called *bon sens*—Cartesian common sense.[21] Common sense concepts are unlike scientific concepts: they are *a priori* rather than artefacts of the discipline. Scientific concepts are made by scientists; they are artefacts, such as the concepts of modern physics: field theory, particles, waves and so on. These are hard-won concepts that took centuries of research and the work of thousands of previous scientists to develop. Nothing like this is true of politics and international relations. Of course, the intelligence agencies have scientific and technical desks whose analysts assess the existence of (say) weapons of mass destruction in Iraq. These analysts do require a relevant technical background. But anyone can understand the social and political implications of these studies if institutions do not work actively to exclude them. Cartesian common sense will suffice.

Ideology

Judgements about national security or foreign affairs rely not so much on expertise as on ideology. It was not that long ago that India—now a great friend and member of the Quad—was regarded as a potential threat to Australia. The first executive director of the Australia Defence Association, Michael O'Connor, explored his own fantasies in *An Act of War* (1990), a novel about a future militaristic India seizing Australian territory in the Indian Ocean.[22] The Cold War had ended and the national security chinstrokers[23] began to look around for new threats. That is what they do, after all. And India was the obvious choice. There was even a superficial plausibility to those judgements. India had leased a nuclear-powered submarine, which it manned and operated for three years. As an Indian rear admiral reflected recently, 'Australian politics and media then had a bogeyman approach to India and the Indian Navy.' Although 'there was no substance to any political/economic threat', some countries might be 'justifiably concerned' because India's defensive capabilities might also be seen as threatening.[24]

When India conducted nuclear tests in 1998, the Howard government recalled its high commissioner to New Delhi and imposed sanctions. The Labor opposition condemned what it called 'an outrageous act of nuclear bastardry'.[25] Australia had an important card to play: it has about 40 per cent of the world's known resources of low-cost uranium. It could deny India uranium exports because India did not sign the Nuclear Non-Proliferation Treaty (NPT). A few years later, the United States changed its export control laws to permit assistance to India's nuclear programs. Labor was in office. The United States asked prime minister Kevin Rudd to support the 'cooperative arrangement with New Delhi'.[26] Six months later, foreign minister Stephen Smith gave a private assurance to his Indian counterpart that Australia would support an exception for the US–India nuclear deal. He confirmed this publicly soon afterwards. In 2016, the Nuclear Power Corporation of India and US-based Westinghouse Corporation agreed to build six nuclear reactors in India. The next year, Australia's first shipment of uranium left for India. This made India the only country in the world to possess nuclear weapons, not be a party to the NPT and still be permitted to engage in nuclear commerce. Today, of course, India is considered a partner with Australia in upholding a 'rules-based international order' in a 'free and open Indo-Pacific'. As one writer has observed, 'Strategic theory and the policy sciences are supple instruments, rarely at a loss to provide the required argument and analysis to buttress the conclusion of the moment.'[27]

Australia and the United States had long been wary of India, as they were of all former colonies after World War II. US officials regarded Indians as 'notably prone to blame others for their problems, as the British know all too well'. They attributed Indian 'ingratitude' to 'a sense of Divine right', which is 'a sort of natural attribute of Indians'. Nehru himself was 'a hypersensitive egoist' who was 'quick to take offence at our slights, real or imagined'.[28] For his part, Australian prime minister Robert Menzies was angered by aspects of Nehru's policy of non-alignment. After one disagreement at the United Nations, Menzies reported that Nehru was 'grossly offensive. All the primitive came out in him.' His attack 'was of the most intemperate kind. He did not revert to the Kashmir Brahmin. He seemed to me to revert almost to the branches of trees.'[29]

But 1950s India could be a counterbalance to China, whose development model, the United States recognised, 'resulted in a rate of economic growth which will probably continue to outstrip that of free Asian countries, with the possible exception of Japan'. China's 'dramatic economic improvements … impress the nations of the region greatly and offer a serious challenge to the Free World'.[30] India did not carry out anti-landlord campaigns in large parts of the countryside, unlike China under Mao. Ugly caste relationships remained. India protected its economy and developed heavy industries but did not seriously threaten social arrangements, especially among the largely rural population. The United States recognised that 'the outcome of the competition between Communist China and India as to which can best satisfy the aspirations of peoples for economic improvement, will have a profound effect throughout Asia and Africa'.[31] Fear of China even then was not sheer fantasy. It was functional; it tracked the outcomes desired by Western policy-makers, namely that former colonies should not challenge local or foreign vested interests in landholdings, plantations, banks, railways, mines, businesses or government debt arrangements.

The different paths chosen by China and India are revealing. When they became independent in the 1940s, both countries were at a broadly similar level: barely above subsistence. India's level of industrialisation and its per capita GDP were slightly higher than China's. But by 1981, according to the World Bank, China had made 'low-income groups far better off in terms of basic needs than their counterparts in most other poor countries'.[32] China's life expectancy, a key indicator of well-being, had overtaken India's. It was well ahead of other low-income countries in per capita energy consumption. Its agricultural production was much higher than India's, and its population was better nourished.[33] Today, India's level of hunger is classified as 'serious' by the Global Hunger Index, which tracks undernourishment and child mortality, child stunting and child wasting in developing countries. (It does not examine high-income countries, where the prevalence of hunger is very low.) India ranks 101st out of 116. China is in the top twenty countries and its level of hunger is classified as 'low'.[34] In 2013, seven major Indian states with a combined population of 545 million were shown to have the same level of multidimensional poverty as the twenty-seven poorest countries of Africa, which had roughly the same population.[35]

Fear of China is not delusional; those who call it a threat can—and usually do—construct a system of beliefs to justify that attitude. They might genuinely believe in the integrity of their position. But lurking in the background is the knowledge that developing countries might emulate the way China controlled the pace, depth and terms of its integration into the international economic system, which is dominated largely by Western investors and the states that act in their interests.[36] China might also develop sufficient military power to retaliate credibly against intimidation. These are not the only reasons for fearing China; it is legitimate and necessary to insist on sovereignty over Australia's telecommunications and other systems for purely defensive reasons. But the imperial factor cannot be stated quite so candidly, perhaps not even to oneself. It must be recast in terms of threat: China's plan for world domination at the head of an international totalitarian wave.

As Andrew Nathan points out in a recent issue of *Foreign Affairs*, China

> has no proposal for an alternative, Beijing-dominated set of institutions. It remains strongly committed to the global free-trade regime, as well as to the UN and that organization's alphabet soup of agencies. It participates actively in the UN human rights system in order to help its allies and frustrate its rivals. Its Belt and Road

> Initiative operates alongside, rather than in place of, long-standing Western-funded development programs.[37]

Nor does it intend to instal 800 military bases in other countries, as the United States has done. But power is relative, and relative to China it is objectively true that the United States is not as powerful as it once was. The subjective reaction to this relative decline is to perceive it as a threat. Likewise, the hostile reactions to China's purchasing food crops from other parts of the world, paying them to divert their agricultural lands to the export sector. These hostile opinions may be genuinely believed because it is second nature to ignore the United States' long history of coups and invasions to subordinate other countries.

One such coup was carried out in Chile by the United States and Australia. In 1971, the Australian Secret Intelligence Service (ASIS) established a 'station' in Santiago, Chile, and conducted clandestine spy operations to provide direct support for US intervention there. The operations destabilised and overthrew the Popular Unity government of Salvador Allende in a military coup on 11 September 1973. The United States' reasons are well known. As President Nixon's national security adviser, Henry Kissinger, warned, 'The example of a successful elected Marxist government in Chile would surely have an impact on—and even precedent value for—other parts of the world, especially in Italy; the imitative spread of similar phenomena elsewhere would in turn significantly affect the world balance and our own position in it.' He admitted that Chile would be 'most likely to appear as an independent socialist country rather than a Soviet satellite or Communist government'. Yet that 'would be far more dangerous to us than it is in Europe' because 'its model effect can be insidious'.[38] The next day, Nixon issued explicit instructions to foment a coup. 'Our main concern,' he said, 'is the prospect that he [Salvador Allende] can consolidate himself and the picture projected to the world will be his success.'[39]

The overthrow of Allende's government resulted in the inauguration of the neoliberal project in Chile: the privatisation of state assets, services and pensions, attacks on organised labour, reduced taxes on the wealthy and on corporations, cutbacks in social welfare schemes and the public sector, and other forms of austerity. The neoliberal project was then implemented in much of the rest of the world in the 1980s and 1990s.[40] It restricted the sovereignty of states and strengthened the interests of private investors, the most dominant of whom came from the USA. That is the rules-based international order in action. ASIS helped begin the global neoliberal class war. It is therefore exempt from an inquiry into its involvement in torture, disappearance and other human rights violations in Chile.[41] These crimes are far from trivial: in a country with a population of 10 million in 1973, there were about 4,000 cases of death or disappearance by the regime, between 150,000 and 200,000 cases of political detention, and approximately 100,000 credible cases of torture.[42]

People who urge respect for a rules-based international order prefer not to discuss Australia's role in the destruction of Chilean democracy. They do not face any direct pressure to stay silent and probably believe everything they say. But if they believed something else, they would not be in those roles. An institutional filtering process selects for those who can internalise the imperial assumptions. Newcomers learn by various cues, explicit and subtle, to avoid certain topics. They begin to conform and to enjoy the privilege of conformity. They soon come to believe what they are saying because it is useful to believe it. Nobody in the system would get anywhere near the higher levels of government unless they already shared the fundamental assumptions.

A related ideological claim is that Australia promotes respect for universal human rights.[43] It certainly does, as do many other countries. But if you want to examine any country's commitment to human rights, the best place to look is where it enjoys an overwhelming advantage in power. Any country can proclaim its dedication to human rights somewhere else in the world. And it can plead inability to act on its high ideals because the world is a difficult, competitive place that makes compromises necessary. But what about where it has an overwhelming amount of influence? There, the usual excuses are absent. That means looking at Australia's record in the south-west Pacific and Timor-Leste—or the US record on human rights in Central America and the Caribbean. In Australia's case, we can ask whether Australia has been a 'good international citizen', in the rhetoric of contemporary cultural management.

We find that Australia has acted as an imperial power. The Department of Foreign Affairs' internal legal advice, as early as February 1975, was that an Indonesian invasion of Timor-Leste, then known as Portuguese Timor, 'would fall into the category of outright aggression'.[44] Aggression, as the Nuremberg Tribunal declared, is 'not only an international crime; it is the supreme international crime differing only from other war crimes in that it contains within itself the accumulated evil of the whole'.[45] The Whitlam government gave Indonesia the green light to invade Timor-Leste. The Fraser government legitimised the occupation by recognising Indonesian sovereignty over the territory and helping it diplomatically when its military operations caused the deaths of about 31 per cent of its population—the largest loss of life relative to total population since World War II.[46] Australian intelligence agencies targeted the survivors and their descendants in espionage and other operations for the purpose of depriving them of control over their sole major natural resource: their oil and gas fields. Bernard Collaery, the lawyer who disclosed one operation, fought in the courts to have his trial conducted in public. In July 2022, the new Attorney-General finally dropped the prosecution against him.

A public trial might show Australians that the espionage operation occurred under cover of an aid project, jeopardising the safety of Australian aid workers everywhere. It also diverted precious ASIS resources away from the war on terrorism. When the ASIS team was in Timor-Leste in September 2004, Jemaah Islamiyah terrorists succeeded in bombing the Australian embassy in Indonesia. The foreign affairs minister at the time of operations against Timor-Leste, Alexander Downer, worked as a lobbyist for Woodside Petroleum after leaving parliament in 2008.[47] The secretary of the Department of Foreign Affairs and Trade, Dr Ashton Calvert, retired and joined the board of directors of Woodside.[48] Professor Andrew Serdy, a former DFAT officer, said: 'Senior officials at all times simply assumed—whether because of direction to that effect by ministers or their offices I do not know—that the national interest was identical to Woodside's.'[49]

The Australian public should not be accused of callous indifference when the ideological institutions deceive them about what happened in Timor-Leste for twenty-four years and what the Australian government did. They do not know, for example, that just an hour's flight from Darwin, East Timorese women were enslaved sexually without fear of reprisal and with the knowledge and complicity of the Indonesian security forces, the civilian administration and members of the judiciary.[50] Australia sent weapons to Indonesia and shielded it from international criticism.[51] Tim Fischer, deputy prime minister in the Howard government, praised Indonesian dictator Suharto as 'perhaps the world's greatest figure in the latter half of the twentieth century'.[52] A bipartisan elite consensus shields foreign policy from public scrutiny, ensuring that it does not enter the terrain of political contestation. Australian public opinion on foreign policy issues is rational in this sense; a valuable study by Caroline Yarnell showed that public opinion responds reasonably to triggers such as international events and statements by political leaders. It is coherent and consistent, showing a degree of structure and discernment.[53] Public opinion reflects Bernard Cohen's observation that the press 'may not be successful much of the time in telling people what to think, but it is stunningly successful in telling its readers what to think *about*'.[54]

The public responds rationally to the facts it sees. Inconvenient facts are not censored but are buried all the same; in principle, they are discoverable, but in reality they are out of the public's awareness because, without regular repetition, no one remembers them. And they have to remain unrepeated and unemphasised precisely because of Australia's democratic freedoms. If they were front and centre, they would never be tolerated by Australians. This is why a former DFAT secretary said, 'We cannot allow foreign policy to be made in the streets, by the media or by the unions.'[55]

A case in point is the public's attitude towards foreign aid. It often hears rhetoric about Australia being too generous with foreign aid: 'Why should billions of taxpayers' dollars be given to overseas countries?' a senator asked. 'The needs of the average Australian family' should take precedence because 'quite simply, charity begins at home'.[56] Quite reasonably, authoritative opinion polls show that Australians think foreign aid spending is too high. They think about 14 per cent of the budget is spent on aid, which was therefore 'the only policy area in which more Australians said that federal government spending should be decreased rather than increased'.[57] When asked, they said only 10 per cent should be spent on aid. The true figure is 0.8 per cent, implying that Australians would support foreign aid spending more than ten times the current figure. The facts of 'boomerang aid' that simply returns to Australian consultants are not part of their awareness. The truth is that Australians are generous, with internationalist tendencies that must be suppressed or kept latent by regular ideological campaigns that make them think money is wasted on foreign countries instead of being spent on needy Australians.

As for government leaders, they probably believe their high-minded rhetoric about dedication to human rights, just as corporate leaders may believe their own professions of commitment to their employees and to human welfare, even as they try to hold down wages and maximise share prices or profits or market share. The question of whether the powerful really believe in their own benevolence is irrelevant as a guide to political action. It might preoccupy writers and others who are entranced by elite sentiment. For those concerned about reforming foreign policy, however, the task is to change the domestic structure of power.

6

Neither their war nor their peace

HOW DOES AUSTRALIAN FOREIGN policy work and for whom? A rich historical record diverges sharply from official pieties. Australia is a subimperial power upholding a US-led imperial order. The euphemism is that it is a middle power trying to uphold a rules-based international order. Whatever term one chooses, the task is to provide an explanatory framework within which that term is defined. That framework must have explanatory adequacy across a wide range of phenomena: Australia's unique economic character; its engagement with international law, human rights, regional diplomacy, arms control, military deployments and weapons purchases; the domestic political structures that enable those external relations.

The explanatory framework of imperialism focuses on the control of other countries' sovereignty. Control can be established by political collaboration between both countries' elites, by economic, social or cultural dependence, by intelligence operations, by the threat or use of force, and sometimes by the physical occupation or annexation of territory. The pay-off is an imperial order known as a rules-based international order, which prioritises the rights of private investors over the sovereignty of most states. It erects a barrier to efforts in developing countries to control the pace, depth and terms of their integration into global markets. The United States and its allies provide the military, financial, diplomatic and other pillars of this order. The doctrine of comparative advantage provides the economic pillar. Belief in imperial benevolence provides the ideological pillar.

Within this framework, Australia is a subimperial power: it is subordinate to the imperial centre, defends the imperial order, and projects considerable power and influence in its own region. To use an analogy from chess, Australia is not a pawn in world affairs. The pawns are vassal states like local clients in Papua New Guinea and elsewhere. Australia joins more powerful pieces on the chessboard in opposing adversaries, maintaining dependence among the pawns, and preventing unity and cooperation among the Global South. This is a large group of lower-income countries that is sometimes called the Third World, the terrain on which the twentieth-century East–West Cold War was waged.[1] An Australian republic would do nothing to change the basic framework of Australian foreign policy. As the philosopher Peter Slezak said,

> Those who have been most passionate about the need to sever purely symbolic ties to Britain have shown no interest in other ties which are arguably more

consequential. The fact that a phone call from the US President has been sufficient to embroil Australia in military interventions around the world has not been seen as evidence of a tie deserving question.[2]

Nothing about these matters is beyond the intellectual capacities of the average person. Policy-makers and other commentators do not possess some special body of impenetrably technical knowledge. People can understand Australia's role in the international arena if institutions do not work actively to exclude them. That calls for long-term collective efforts to reveal rather than mystify Australian foreign policy. It requires acknowledgement that the 'rules-based' imperial order and the policies that uphold it have delivered benefits to Australia. Immigrants from around the world are drawn to Australia because it remains a prosperous, peaceful, free, democratic country. Things are very different for those on the receiving end of imperialism. As foreign minister Paul Hasluck said in the 1960s, 'In Australia we are content with the existing international order ... It is easier for us to be virtuous than it is for some others because the course of virtue coincides with our self-interest.' But many countries 'are not so pleased with the existing order as we are. Some of them only became nations after the existing order had been established, and they had no part in saying anything about the sort of world into which they were born.' He warned, 'We cannot just try to hold down the lid of a boiling pot by placing a ton of principles on top of it in the blind belief that nothing is going to happen.' Rather, there should be 'change by a peaceful process in a way conformable to the needs and interests of nations, though not in disregard of vital principles'.[3]

The world after the Ukraine crisis presents new challenges for Australian foreign policy. Few countries in the Global South have joined the campaign of economic sanctions against Russia. A commentator who spoke with diplomats and analysts from across Africa, Asia, the Middle East and Latin America reported that 'these countries largely sympathize with the plight of the Ukrainian people and view Russia as the aggressor' but that 'Western demands that they make costly sacrifices ... to uphold a "rules-based order" have begotten an allergic reaction'. As they see it, '[N]o other country or bloc has undermined international law, norms or the rules-based order more than the US and the West.' Invasions, war crimes, coups, sanctions and other acts have usually been directed against the Global South. To demand that they make massive and costly sacrifices to uphold 'an order in which the US can continue to act outside international law is equivalent to asking the Global South to make unbearable sacrifices to uphold American exceptionalism'.[4]

Australia will align reflexively with the United States and its allies, but much of the world might want neither war nor an unjust peace; neutrality is becoming a serious option. Once known as non-alignment, a version of it is likely to resurface in calls for a multipolar world. This world has been a decade in the making. The concept of a Democratic, Equitable International Order has been discussed at the United Nations every year since 2011 but has never been discussed or reported seriously in the Australian media.[5] A democratic, equitable, international order would be an alternative to an imperial order whether led by the United States or a China-based alliance system. Given the military and financial strength of the United States, Australia is unlikely to make a serious commitment to neutrality, multipolarity or a democratic and equitable international order. Its organising principle is to stay on the winning side of the global contest between developed and developing countries. But this stance will run up against China's outreach to the developing world while the United States faces a deeply polarised political landscape and the prospect of democratic erosion.[6]

Notes

INTRODUCTION

1 Department of Foreign Affairs and Trade, *In the National Interest*, Commonwealth of Australia, 1997, p. iii.
2 G. Evans, *Making Australian Foreign Policy*, Australian Fabian Society, pamphlet no. 50, 1989.
3 T. Plibersek, 'National interest, good international citizenship and Labor's foreign policy', Lowy Institute, 31 May 2016.
4 J. Frydenberg, 'The Liberal tradition in Australian foreign policy', in A. Carr, A.J. Langlois and D. Baldino (eds), *Australian Foreign Policy: Controversies and Debates*, Oxford University Press, South Melbourne, 2014, pp. 21–8.
5 R. Maude, 'The rules-based international order and the Foreign Policy White Paper', in M. Conley Tyler, A. Gyngell and B. Wakefield (eds), *Australia and the Rules-based International Order*, Australian Institute of International Affairs, Deakin, 2021, pp. 43–56.
6 M.W. Doyle, *Empires*, Cornell University Press, Ithaca, 1986, p. 45.

7 K. Lascurettes, *Orders of Exclusion: Great Powers and the Strategic Sources of Foundational Rules in International Relations*, Oxford University Press, New York, 2020, p. 32.

8 L. Reddick, 'Africa: Test of the Atlantic Charter', *Crisis*, vol. 50, no. 7, 1943, pp. 202–18.

9 G. Kolko, *The Politics of War: The World and United States Foreign Policy, 1943–1945*, Pantheon, New York, 1968; B. Davidson, *Scenes from the Anti-Nazi War*, Monthly Review, New York, 1980; L. Wittner, *American Intervention in Greece, 1943–1949*, Columbia University Press, New York, 1982; F. Romero, *The United States and the European Trade Union Movement, 1944–1951*, University of North Carolina Press, Chapel Hill, 1992; A. Cockburn and J. St Clair, *Whiteout: The CIA, Drugs, and the Press*, Verso, London, 1999, chapters 5–7.

10 S. Wertheim, 'Instrumental internationalism: The American origins of the United Nations, 1940–3', *Journal of Contemporary History*, vol. 54, no. 2, 2019, pp. 265–83.

11 D. Cave, 'Australia may well be the world's most secretive democracy', *New York Times*, 5 June 2019.

1 A SUBIMPERIAL POWER

1 Joint Statement on Australia–US Ministerial Consultations (AUSMIN) 2021, www.state.gov/joint-statement-on-australia-u-s-ministerial-consultations-ausmin-2021

2 L. Frederickson, 'The development of Australian infantry on the Western Front 1916–1918: An imperial model of training, tactics and technology', PhD thesis, UNSW Canberra, 2015, p. 135.

3 Ibid., p. 135.

4 Ibid., p. 135.
5 B. Dyster and D. Meredith, *Australia in the Global Economy: Continuity and Change*, 3rd edn, Cambridge University Press, Melbourne, 2012, p. 61.
6 K. Willey, 'Australia's population', *Labour History*, vol. 35, issue 1, 1978, pp. 1–9.
7 J. Jupp, *The English in Australia*, Cambridge University Press, Cambridge, 2004, p. 1.
8 C. Storr, '"Imperium in imperio": Sub-imperialism and the formation of Australia as a subject of international law', *Melbourne Journal of International Law*, vol. 19, no. 1, 2018; R.C. Thompson, *Australian Imperialism in the Pacific: The Expansionist Era 1820–1920*, Melbourne University Press, Carlton, 1980; H. McQueen, *A New Britannia*, 4th edn, University of Queensland Press, St Lucia, 2004, pp. 50–6.
9 Australian Bureau of Statistics, 'Migration, 2019–20 financial year', 23 April 2021, www.abs.gov.au/statistics/people/population/migration-australia/2019-20
10 B. Nicholson (US Army Pacific Commander), 'Next war will be violent, very human, unpredictable and long', *ASPI Strategist*, 18 February 2022.
11 Doyle, *Empires*, p. 45.
12 J. Caesar, *The Conquest of Gaul*, trans. S.A. Handford, Penguin Books, Harmondsworth, 1953, p. 130.
13 Emphasis in the original. W.V. Harris, *War and Imperialism in Republican Rome, 327–70 BC*, Oxford University Press, Oxford, 1985, p. 105.
14 Ibid., p. 106.
15 W. Stivers, *Supremacy and Oil*, Cornell University Press, Ithaca, 1982, pp. 15, 34.

16 G. Kennan, *American Diplomacy 1900–1950*, University of Chicago Press, Chicago, 1951, p. 5.

17 R. O'Rourke, 'US role in the world', 19 January 2021, p. 4, https://crsreports.congress.gov/product/details?prodcode=R44891; 'Renewed great power competition', 10 March 2022, p. 5, https://crsreports.congress.gov/product/details?prodcode=R43838.

18 J. Stoltenberg, 'Remarks to Donald Trump', 11 July 2018, www.nato.int/cps/en/natohq/opinions_156854.htm

19 D. MacArthur, 'Memorandum on Formosa, 14 June 1950', *Foreign Relations of the United States 1950*, vol. VII, Korea, https://history.state.gov/historicaldocuments/frus1950v07/d86

20 E. Ratner, 'Statement before the United States Senate Committee on Foreign Relations', 8 December 2021.

21 J.S. Marcus, N. Poitiers and P. Weil, 'The decoupling of Russia: Software, media and online services', Bruegel Blog, 22 March 2022.

22 'Why China's payment system can't easily save Russian banks cut off from Swift', Bloomberg Quicktake, 15 March 2022 www.bloomberg.com/news/articles/2022-03-14/why-china-s-payment-system-can-t-easily-save-russia-quicktake

23 P. Dutton, National Press Club address, Canberra, 26 November 2021.

24 L. O'Rourke, *Covert Regime Change*, Cornell University Press, Ithaca, 2018.

25 Ibid., p. 75.

26 F. Costigliola, 'The pursuit of Atlantic community: Nuclear arms, dollars, and Berlin', in T.G. Paterson (ed.), *Kennedy's Quest for Victory: American Foreign Policy, 1961–1963*, Oxford University Press, New York, 1989, pp. 27–8.

27 S. Kuper, 'What happens when elites abandon their homeland', *Financial Times*, 29 July 2021. Data from www.theglobaleconomy.com/rankings/human_flight_brain_drain_index

28 N. Kassam, Lowy Institute Poll, 2021, https://poll.lowyinstitute.org/report/2021.

29 P. Wintour, 'US seen as bigger threat to democracy than Russia or China, global poll finds', *Guardian*, 5 May 2021.

30 Kassam, Lowy Institute Poll, 2021.

31 Document 298 in R. Bowker and M. Jordan (eds), *Australia and the Suez Crisis 1950–1957*, UNSW Press & Australian Department of Foreign Affairs and Trade, Sydney, 2021.

32 W. Hudson, *Blind Loyalty: Australia and the Suez Crisis, 1956*, Melbourne University Press, Carlton, 1989, pp. 8–9.

33 Reserve Bank of Australia, *Occasional Paper No. 8: Australian Economic Statistics 1949–1950 to 1996–1997*.

34 Kassam, Lowy Institute Poll, 2021.

35 J. Gillard, Speech to US Congress, 9 March 2011.

36 K. Rudd, 'Australia, the United States and the Asia Pacific region', speech to the Brookings Institution, 31 March 2008.

37 B. Scott, 'Rules-based order: What's in a name?', Lowy Institute, 30 June 2021.

38 J. Grey, *A Military History of Australia*, 3rd edn, Cambridge University Press, Melbourne, 2008, p. 8.

39 C. Ungerer, 'The "middle power" concept in Australian foreign policy', *Australian Journal of Politics and History*, vol. 53, no. 4, 2007, pp. 538–51.

40 P. Hartcher, 'Julie Bishop: A firm gaze and straight talk from an unflappable foreign minister', *Sydney Morning Herald* [henceforth SMH], 15 August 2014.

41 A. Downer, 'Should Australia think big or small in foreign policy?', Centre for Independent Studies, 10 July 2006.
42 This approach is well understood in the history and philosophy of knowledge. Even in mathematics, the most formal of disciplines, the concept of 'limit' was unclear until the framework of calculus was developed.
43 J.A. Schumpeter, *The Theory of Economic Development*, Harvard University Press, Cambridge, MA, 1934, pp. 273–4.
44 C.A. Hidalgo, R. Hausmann and P.S. Dasgupta, 'The building blocks of economic complexity', *Proceedings of the National Academy of Sciences of the United States of America*, vol. 106, no. 26, 2009, pp. 10570–5.
45 Growth Lab at Harvard University, *The Atlas of Economic Complexity*, www.atlas.cid.harvard.edu.
46 Office of the Chief Economist, 'Globalizing Australia', *Industry Insights*, June 2018.
47 P. Hasluck, 'Australian foreign policy', *Current Notes on International Affairs*, vol. 38, no. 1, 1967.
48 Data collected in March and April 2022. I thank UNSW Canberra's Research Infrastructure Scheme for providing access to the Bloomberg Terminal, which contains geographical data on corporate ownership based on live purchases and sales.
49 Senate Economics Committee, 'Greenfields, cash cows and the regulation of foreign investment in Australia', Parliament of Australia, August 2021, pp. 43–5.
50 N. Phillips, 'Power and inequality in the global political economy', *International Affairs*, vol. 93, no. 2, 2017, pp. 429–44.
51 United Nations Conference on Trade and Development (UNCTAD), 'Global value chains: Investment and trade

for development', *World Investment Report 2013*, Geneva, 2013, p. x.

52 'Australia trade policy update: Beef decision close?', 09CANBERRA281_a, 23 March 2009, via WikiLeaks, https://wikileaks.org/plusd/cables/09CANBERRA281_a.html

53 N. Tarrant, *IBISWorld Industry Report C2394: Aircraft Manufacturing and Repair Services in Australia*, December 2017.

54 W. Hudson and M. Sharpe, *Australian Independence: Colony to a Reluctant Kingdom*, Melbourne University Press, Carlton, 1988, pp. 8–9.

55 Dyster and Meredith, *Australia in the Global Economy*.

56 Covering Clause 5, sections 73 and 74. The *Australia Act 1986* (Cwlth) made significant changes.

57 Hudson and Sharpe, *Australian Independence*.

58 *Brown v. West* [1990] HCA 7; 169 CLR 195, 1 March 1990, High Court of Australia, www.austliiedu.au/au/cases/cth/HCA/1990/7.html

59 Joint Standing Committee on Treaties, Report 26: *An Agreement to Extend the Period of Operation of the Joint Defence Facility at Pine Gap*, 1999, pp. 6–10.

60 *Intelligence Services Act 2001* (Cwlth), section 29.

61 Senator R. Patrick, Second reading speech, *Hansard*, 14 August 2018, pp. 4688–92.

62 J. Curran, 'Canberra's wolverines threaten our connection to the region', *Australian Financial Review*, 8 May 2020.

63 A. Palazzo, 'The future of war debate in Australia: Why has there not been one? Has the need for one now arrived?', Land Warfare Studies Centre Working Paper No. 140, August 2012.

64 P. Leahy, 'Combat ready?', in T. Frame and A. Palazzo (eds), *On Ops: Lessons and Challenges for the Australian Army since East Timor*, NewSouth, Sydney, 2016, p. 51; J. Blaxland, *The Australian Army from Whitlam to Howard*, Cambridge University Press, Port Melbourne, 2014.

2 THE RULES-BASED INTERNATIONAL ORDER

1 US Department of State, Transcript of Meeting, Anchorage, Alaska, 18 March 2021; www.state.gov/secretary-antony-j-blinken-national-security-advisor-jake-sullivan-chinese-director-of-the-office-of-the-central-commission-for-foreign-affairs-yang-jiechi-and-chinese-state-councilor-wang-yi-at-th/

2 W. Hastings, letter to the Court of Directors of the British East India Company, 3 November 1772, Appendix A, 'Bengal portrayed in 1772', in W.W. Hunter, *The Annals of Rural Bengal*, Smith, Elder & Co., London, 1868, p. 381.

3 W. Dalrymple, *The Anarchy: The Relentless Rise of the East India Company*, Bloomsbury, New Delhi, 2019, p. xxxiii.

4 J. Broadbent, S. Rickard and M. Steven, *India, China, Australia: Trade and Society 1788–1850*, Historic Houses Trust, Sydney, 2003, pp. 9–10. D. Walker, *Anxious Nation: Australia and the Rise of Asia 1850–1939*, University of Queensland Press, Brisbane, 1999, p. 13.

5 Walker, *Anxious Nation*, p. 13.

6 Dyster and Meredith, *Australia in the Global Economy*, p. 61.

7 U. Patnaik, 'Revisiting the "drain", or transfers from India to Britain', in S. Chakravarti and U. Patnaik (eds), *Agrarian*

and Other Histories: Essays for Binay Bhushan Chaudhuri, Tulika Books, New Delhi, 2017, pp. 278–317.

8 A.K. Bagchi, 'Some international foundations of capitalist growth and underdevelopment', *Economic and Political Weekly*, August 1972.

9 L. Davis and R. Huttenback, *Mammon and the Pursuit of Empire: The Political Economy of British Imperialism, 1860–1912*, Cambridge University Press, New York, 1987, p. 163.

10 I. Habib, 'Studying a colonial economy—without perceiving colonialism', *Modern Asian Studies*, vol. 19, no. 3, 1985, pp. 355–81; M. Davis, *Late Victorian Holocausts: El Niño Famines and the Making of the Third World*, Verso, London, 2002, pp. 311–12.

11 A. Deakin, *Temple and Tomb in India*, Melville, Mullen & Slade, Melbourne, 1893, pp. 129–30.

12 M. Moynagh, *Brown or White? A History of the Fiji Sugar Industry, 1873–1973*, Australian National University, Canberra, 1981.

13 H. Tinker, *A New System of Slavery: The Export of Indian Labour Overseas, 1830–1920s*, Oxford University Press, London, 1974.

14 C. Markovits, *A History of Modern India, 1480–1950*, Anthem Press, London, 2004, p. 289.

15 J. Sassoon, *The Global Merchants: The Enterprise and Extravagance of the Sassoon Dynasty*, Allen Lane, London, 2022.

16 J. Seeley, *The Expansion of England*, Macmillan, London, 1886.

17 J. Grey, 'In every war but one? Myth, history and Vietnam', in C. Stockings (ed.), *Zombie Myths of Australian Military History*, UNSW Press, Sydney, 2010, p. 192.

18 J.S. Mill [1859], 'A few words on non-intervention', *Fraser's Magazine*, reprinted in *New England Review*, vol. 27, no. 3, 2006, pp. 252–64.

19 R.K. Newman, 'Opium smoking in late imperial China: A reconsideration', *Modern Asian Studies*, vol. 29, no. 4, 1995, p. 787.

20 D. Peers, *India under Colonial Rule: 1700–1885*, Routledge, London, 2006, p. 64.

21 L. Nayder, 'Class consciousness and the Indian Mutiny in Dickens' "The Perils of Certain English Prisoners"', *Studies in English Literature, 1500–1900*, vol. 32, no. 4, 1992, pp. 689–705.

22 C. Elkins, *Legacy of Violence: A History of the British Empire*, Knopf, New York, 2022.

23 Prime Minister Harold Holt MP's audience with Prince Sihanouk, April 1967, NAA: A1209, 1966/7112A.

24 R. Shaplen, *The Lost Revolution: The US in Vietnam, 1946–1966*, Harper & Row, New York, 1966, pp. 104, 114–15.

25 L. Bourke, 'John Howard "embarrassed" by failed WMD intelligence on Iraq', *SMH*, 22 September 2014.

26 A. Smith, *An Inquiry into the Nature and Causes of the Wealth of Nations*, Book 2, chapter 5, University of Chicago Press, Chicago, 1977, pp. 486–7.

27 P. Bairoch, *Economics and World History*, University of Chicago Press, Chicago, 1993.

28 J. Bowring, *Report on Egypt and Candia*, W. Clowes & Sons, London, 1840.

29 A.L. al-Sayyid Marsot, *A History of Egypt*, Cambridge University Press, Cambridge, 2007, p. 77.
30 J. Hickel, *The Divide*, Windmill Books, London, 2018.
31 B. Davidson, *The Black Man's Burden*, James Currey, London, 1992.
32 C. Stockings, 'Other people's wars', in C. Stockings (ed.), *Anzac's Dirty Dozen: 12 Myths of Australian Military History*, NewSouth Publishing, Sydney, 2012, pp. 75–99.
33 C. Buckley and D. Cave, 'Australia took on China. Did it get it right?', *New York Times*, 6 October 2021.
34 M. Klare, 'None dare call it "encirclement"', TomDispatch.com, 13 January 2022.
35 P. Dorling, 'Desert secrets', *SMH*, 21 July 2013.
36 B. Toohey, *Secret: The Making of Australia's Security State*, Melbourne University Press, Carlton, 2019.
37 S. Smith, 'Ministerial statement', House of Representatives, Canberra, 26 June 2013.
38 R. Bernhardt, *Encyclopedia of Public International Law: Use of Force, War and Neutrality*, vol. 4: 'Use of force, war, and neutrality peace treaties' (N–Z), North Holland Publishing Company, Amsterdam, 1982, p. 22.
39 K. Beazley, John Curtin Anniversary Lecture, 6 December 2021, https://jcpml.curtin.edu.au/events/anniversary-lectures/
40 N. Hulme, 'China consortium wins rights to develop Guinea iron ore deposit', *Financial Times*, 2 December 2019.
41 D. Crowe, 'China warning: Joyce calls on MPs to prepare for end of Pax Americana', *SMH*, 22 June 2021.
42 M. Cordell, 'Three West Papuans occupy Australian consulate in Bali', *Guardian*, 6 October 2013.

43 P. Doulman, 'Tony Abbott's claim West Papua "getting better" rejected by experts', *SMH*, 9 October 2013.
44 E. Bagshaw, 'Tony Abbott, in Taipei, says it's time to end Taiwan's isolation', *SMH*, 7 October 2021.
45 P. Dorling (ed.), Document 82, *Diplomasi: Australia and Indonesia's Independence*, DFAT, 1994.
46 A. Jackson, 'On a mission to sway Australia's view', *Age*, 18 September 2006.
47 Bloomberg Professional Terminal searches conducted in March and April 2022.
48 J. Thornhill, H. Lun and S. Ahn, 'Billionaire miner sees next fortune in rush for clean energy', Bloomberg, 14 October 2021.
49 R.G. Skirrow, D.L. Huston, T.P. Mernagh, J.P. Thorne, H. Dulfer and A.B. Senior, 'Critical commodities for a high-tech world: Australia's potential to supply global demand', Geoscience Australia, 2013, www.ga.gov.au/data-pubs/data-and-publications-search/publications/critical-commodities-for-a-high-tech-world.
50 G. Myrdal, *Economic Theory and Under-developed Regions*, Methuen, London, 1963.
51 A. Beattie, 'The EU plan to live in a raw materials world', *Financial Times*, 26 November 2020.
52 T. Riofrancos, *Resource Radicals: From Petro-nationalism to Post-extractivism in Ecuador*, Duke University Press, Durham, 2020.
53 M.P. Mills, 'Mines, minerals, and "green" energy: A reality check', Manhattan Institute, July 2020.
54 G. Rundle, 'Requiem for a panda father', *Crikey*, 30 March 2022.

55 T. Lester, 'Israel responsible for faking Aussie passports, diplomat expelled: Smith', *SMH*, 24 May 2010.

56 K. Rudd, *Kevin Rudd: The PM Years*, Pan Macmillan, Sydney, 2018.

57 US State Department, 'Despite passport incident, probably "No" vote on Goldstone', Cable 10CANBERRA137_a, 25 February2010, https://wikileaks.org/plusd/cables/10CANBERRA137_a.html

58 B. Beit-Hallahmi, *The Israeli Connection: Who Israel Arms and Why*, Pantheon Books, New York, 1987; J. Hunter, *Israeli Foreign Policy: South Africa and Central America*, South End Press, Boston, 1987.

59 E.-I. Dovere, 'Biden: Always Israel's friend', *Politico*, 30 September 2013.

60 J. Sharp, J. Zanotti, K. Katzman, C. Arabia and C. Thomas, *Israel's Qualitative Military Edge and Possible US Arms Sales to the United Arab Emirates*, Congressional Research Service, 26 October 2020.

61 C. Halle, 'Envoy to Australia to explain "yellow race" comments', *Ha'aretz*, 16 October 2006.

62 Human Rights Watch, 'A threshold crossed: Israeli authorities and the crimes of apartheid and persecution', April 2021, www.hrw.org; Amnesty International, 'Israel's apartheid against Palestinians: Cruel system of domination and crime against humanity', February 2022, www.amnesty.org/en/documents/mde15/5141/2022/en/; B'TSelem—The Israeli Information Center for Human Rights in the Occupied Territories, 'A regime of Jewish supremacy from the Jordan River to the Mediterranean Sea: This is apartheid', January 2021, www.btselem.org/publications/fulltext/202101_this_is_apartheid

63 DFAT, 'Australia and Timor-Leste maritime boundaries: Rules-based order in action', media release, March 2018 (retrieved 10 March 2022), www.internationalaffairs.org.au/wp-content/uploads/2021/10/Australia-and-the-Rules-Based-International-Order.pdf

64 White House, *National Security Strategy of the United States*, September 2002. https://georgewbush-whitehouse.archives.gov/nsc/nss/2002/

65 M. Albright, 'Bridges, bombs or bluster?', *Foreign Affairs*, vol. 82, issue 5, 2003, pp. 2–19.

66 R. Oppel, 'Early target of offensive is a hospital', *New York Times*, 8 November 2004.

67 R. Tanter, D. Ball and G. van Klinken, *Masters of Terror: Indonesia's Military and Violence in East Timor*, Rowman & Littlefield, Lanham, 2006.

68 UN Office of the High Commissioner for Human Rights, Report of the International Commission of Inquiry on East Timor, 31 January 2000, A/54/726, S/2000/59.

69 G. Till, 'Outgoing Australia?', Centre of Gravity Series No. 14, Strategic and Defence Studies Centre, ANU, Canberra, 2014, p. 5.

3 AUKUS

1 D. Dickens, 'The United Nations in East Timor: Intervention at the military operational level', *Contemporary Southeast Asia*, vol. 23, no. 2, 2001, p. 224.

2 A. Palazzo, 'Planning to not lose: The Australian Army's new philosophy of war', Australian Army Occasional Paper No. 3, Australian Army Research Centre, 2021.

3 D. Johnston, *The Importance of the Future Submarine for Australia: The Submarine Choice*, Australian Strategic Policy Institute, Canberra, 2014.

4 J. Goldrick, 'Submarine acquisition in Australia', in G. Till and C. Koh Swee Lean (eds), *Naval Modernisation in Southeast Asia*, Part 2: *Submarine Issues for Small and Medium Navies*, Palgrave Macmillan, Cham, 2019.

5 B. Toohey, *Secret: The Making of Australia's Security State*, Melbourne University Press, Carlton, 2019.

6 M. Smith, 'China to ramp up oil, gas, coal production', *Australian Financial Review*, 7 March 2022.

7 'On the defence', *Utopia*, 2017, www.imdb.com/title/tt7034282

8 E. Slavin, 'Chinese admiral contests freedom of navigation in South China Sea', *Stars and Stripes*, 19 July 2016.

9 P.A. Dutton (US Naval War College), Testimony before the US–China Economic and Security Review Committee Hearing on the Implications of China's Naval Modernization for the United States, 11 June 2009.

10 US 7th Fleet Public Affairs, 'US 7th Fleet conducts freedom of navigation operation', 7 April 2021, www.c7f.navy.mil/Media/News/Display/Article/2563538/7th-fleet-conducts-freedom-of-navigation-operation

11 R. Pandit, 'In unusual move, US Navy conducts operation near Lakshadweep without India's consent', *Times of India*, 10 April 2021.

12 This section draws on my chapter in Emma Dawson and Janet McCalman (eds), *What Happens Next? Reconstructing Australia After COVID-19*, Melbourne University Press Digital, 2020.

13 D. Rodrik, 'What do trade agreements really do?', *Journal of Economic Perspectives*, vol. 32, no. 2, 2018, pp. 73–90.

14 Ibid, p. 75.

15 H.V.J. Moir, 'The patent price of market access in the AUSFTA', *Australian Journal of International Affairs*, vol. 69, no. 5, 2015, pp. 559–76.

16 H. Moir, 'Do patent systems improve economic well-being? An exploration of the inventiveness of business method patents', PhD diss., Australian National University, 2008, p. 53.

17 H. Moir, *Patent Policy and Innovation: Do Legal Rules Deliver Effective Outcomes?*, Edward Elgar, Cheltenham, 2013, p. 57.

18 'GOA rejects proposal to manufacture generic drugs for export', 09CANBERRA686_a, 27 July 2009, via WikiLeaks, https://wikileaks.org/plusd/cables/09CANBERRA686a.html

19 H.V.J. Moir, 'Reviewing patent policy: An exercise in futility?', *Prometheus*, vol. 33, no. 4, 2015, pp. 431–43.

20 E. Humphrys, *How Labour Built Neoliberalism*, Brill, Leiden, 2018; D. Cahill and P. Toner (eds), *Wrong Way: How Privatisation and Economic Reform Backfired*, La Trobe University Press, Melbourne, 2018.

21 C. Hamilton and J. Quiggin, *The Privatisation of CSL*, Discussion Paper No. 4, June 1995, Australia Institute, Deakin, ACT.

22 B. Lokuge and C. Hamilton, *Comparing Drug Prices in Australia and the USA: The Implications of the US–Australia Free Trade Agreement*, Australia Institute, July 2003, https://australiainstitute.org.au/report/comparing-

drug-prices-in-australia-and-the-usa-the-implications-of-the-us-australia-free-trade-agreement/

23 'Australian health care: An overview', 09CANBERRA464_a, 17 May 2009, https://search.wikileaks.org/plusd/cables/09CANBERRA464_a.html

24 C. Lawson, 'Quantum of obviousness in Australian patent laws', *Australian Intellectual Property Journal*, vol. 19, 2003, pp. 43–65.

25 A. Richardson, 'Pharmaceutical product manufacturing in Australia', *IBISWorld Industry Report C1841*, February 2022, p. 20.

26 DFAT, *Trade and Investment at a Glance 2020*, Department of Foreign Affairs and Trade, Canberra, 2020.

27 Philip Morris Asia Limited, 'Written Notification of Claim, 27 June 2011' (retrieved 10 March 2022), www.ag.gov.au/Internationalrelations/InternationalLaw/Documents/Philip-Morris-Asia-Limited-Notice-of-Claim-27-June-2011.pdf

28 Coalition 2013 election policy, *The Coalition's Policy for Trade*, Coalition, September 2013, https://lpaweb-static.s3.amazonaws.com/Coalition%202013%20Election%20Policy%20%E2%80%93%20Trade%20%E2%80%93%20final.pdf

29 P. Kornbluh, *Australian Spies Aided and Abetted CIA in Chile*, National Security Archive, 10 September 2021, https://nsarchive.gwu.edu/briefing-book/chile/2021-09-10/australian-spies-aided-and-abetted-cia-chile

30 J. Bonnitcha, L. Poulsen and M. Waibel, *The Political Economy of the Investment Treaty Regime*, Oxford University Press, Oxford, 2017, p. 12.

31 J. Williamson (ed.), *Latin American Adjustment: How Much Has Happened*, Institute for international Economics, Washington DC, 1990, chapter 2, pp. 5–21.
32 C. Merritt, 'Money men', *Australian Legal Review*, 26 October 2018, p. 26.
33 *Movitor v. Sims* [1996] FCA 205; 136 ALR 643; 14 ACLC 587; 19 ACSR 440; *Campbells Cash and Carry v. Fostif* [2006] HCA 41; 229 CLR 386; 80 ALJR 1441; 229 ALR 58.
34 Bonnitcha, Poulsen and Waibel, *The Political Economy of the Investment Treaty Regime*, p. 69.
35 Ibid., p. 199.

4 THE CHINA DIVIDE

1 B. Davis and J. Hilsenrath, 'How the China shock, deep and swift, spurred the rise of Trump', *Wall Street Journal*, 11 August 2016.
2 Defence Strategic Update 2020, p. 15, www.defence.gov.au/about/publications/2020-defence-strategic-update
3 Newman, 'Opium smoking in late imperial China: A reconsideration', p. 787.
4 A.S. Lindemann, *Esau's Tears: Modern Anti-Semitism and the Rise of the Jews*, Cambridge University Press, Cambridge, 1997, pp. 507–10.
5 W.A. Callahan, *China: The Pessoptimist Nation*, Oxford University Press, Oxford, 2010, p. 193.
6 A.J. Nathan and A. Scobell, *China's Search for Security*, Columbia University Press, New York, 2012, p. 17.
7 Ibid., p. 17.

8 Portrait of Vice President Xi Jinping: 'Ambitious survivor' of the Cultural Revolution, 09BEIJING3128_a, 16 November 2009, https://search.wikileaks.org/plusd/cables/09BEIJING3128_a.html
9 E. Economy, 'Xi Jinping's new world order', *Foreign Affairs*, vol. 101, no. 1, 2022, pp. 52–67.
10 A. Macias and K. Tausche, 'US needs to work with Europe to slow China's innovation rate, Raimondo says', CNBC, 28 September 2021.
11 D. Byler, *In the Camps: China's High-tech Penal Colony*, Columbia University Global Reports, 2021.
12 J. Seaman, 'China and the new geopolitics of technical standardisation', French Institute of International Relations, January 2020, p. 6. See also P. Cai, *Understanding China's Belt and Road Initiative*, Lowy Institute, Sydney, 2017.
13 J. Kynge and N. Liu, 'From AI to facial recognition: How China is setting the rules in new tech', *Financial Times*, 7 October 2020.
14 Davis and Hilsenrath, 'How the China shock, deep and swift, spurred the rise of Trump'.
15 M. Sheehan, 'The Chinese way of innovation', *Foreign Affairs*, 21 April 2022, www.foreignaffairs.com/articles/china/2022-04-21/chinese-way-innovation
16 E. Barrett, 'China will spend $300 billion on semiconductor imports as US squeezes chip supply', *Fortune*, 27 August 2020.
17 President's Council of Advisors on Science and Technology, *Report to the President: Ensuring Long-Term US Leadership in Semiconductors*, Washington, DC, January 2017, www.whitehouse.gov/sites/default/files/microsites/ostp/PCAST/

pcast_ensuring_long-term_us_leadership_in_semiconductors.pdf

18 K. Friis and O. Lysne, 'Huawei, 5G and security: Technological limitations and political responses', *Development and Change*, vol. 52, no. 5, pp. 1174–95.

19 Computer Network Exploitation Classification Guide/2-59 [online], www.spiegel.de/media/media-35656.pdf

20 D. Ben-Atar, *Trade Secrets: Intellectual Piracy and the Origins of American Industrial Power*, Yale University Press, New Haven, 2004, p. 148.

21 Ibid., p. 35.

22 M. Wilkins, *The History of Foreign Investment in the United States, 1914–1945*, Harvard University Press, Cambridge, 2004, p. 122.

23 N. Yau and D. van der Kley, 'China's global network of vocational colleges to train the world', *Diplomat*, 11 November 2021, https://thediplomat.com/2021/11/chinas-global-network-of-vocational-colleges-to-train-the-world

24 E. Cunningham, T. Saich and J. Turiel, 'Understanding CCP resilience: Surveying Chinese public opinion through time', Ash Center for Democratic Governance and Innovation, Kennedy School, Harvard University, July 2020.

25 E. White and V. Mallet, 'How Xi Jinping's anti-corruption crusade went global', *Financial Times*, 22 February 2022.

26 D. Stanway and S.-L. Wong, 'Smog may be easing, but in parts of China water quality worsens', Reuters, 18 November 2016.

27 Australia Institute, *Climate of the Nation 2019*, December 2019; 'Is the public willing to pay to help fix climate change?', Energy Policy Institute and Associated Press—NORC

Center for Public Affairs Research, https://epic.uchicago.edu/wp-content/uploads/2019/08/AP-NORC-2019-Fact-Sheet.pdf

28 C. Heurlin, *Responsive Authoritarianism in China*, Cambridge University Press, Cambridge, 2016.

29 'China and Coronashock', Tricontinental: Institute for Social Research, 28 April 2020.

30 M. Tischler, 'China's "never again" mentality', *Diplomat*, 18 August 2020, https://thediplomat.com/2020/08/chinas-never-again-mentality

31 A.-M. Brady, *Marketing Dictatorship: Propaganda and Thought Work in Contemporary China*, Rowman & Littlefield, Lanham, 2009, p. 69.

32 A.J. Nathan, 'Medals and rights', *New Republic*, 9 July 2008.

33 E. Williams, *British Historians in the West Indies*, André Deutsch, London, 1966, p. 233.

34 L. Silver, K. Devlin and C. Huang, 'Unfavorable views of China reach historic highs in many countries', Pew Research Center, 6 October 2020.

35 S.L. Myers, 'With ships and missiles, China is ready to challenge US Navy in Pacific', *New York Times*, 29 August 2018.

36 J. Greber, M. Smith and A. Tillett, 'Canberra plans for Taiwan conflict', *Australian Financial Review*, 17 April 2021.

37 K. Hille, 'TSMC: How a Taiwanese chipmaker became a linchpin of the global economy', *Financial Times*, 25 March 2021.

38 L. Henley, 'Testimony before the US–China Economic and Security Review Commission Hearing on Cross-strait

Deterrence', 18 February 2021, https://www.uscc.gov/sites/default/files/2021-02/Lonnie_Henley_Testimony.pdf

39 06CANBERRA1366, 'Ambassador's introductory call on opposition', 8 September 2006, http://wikileaks.wikimee.org/cable/2006/09/06CANBERRA1366.html

40 06CANBERRA1517_a, 'Opposition leader Beazley will fight PM Howard for the political center', 26 September 2006, https://search.wikileaks.org/plusd/cables/06CANBERRA1517_a.html

41 T. Bramston, 'Taiwan defence a must: Dutton', *Australian*, 13 November 2021.

42 D.C. Gompert, A.S. Cevallos and C.L. Garafola, *War with China: Thinking through the Unthinkable*, RAND Corporation, Santa Monica, 2016.

43 C. Rovere, 'A review of RAND's war with China: Thinking through the unthinkable', Lowy Institute, 24 August 2016.

44 L. de Wei, 'Why the Solomon Islands' China pact has US riled', Bloomberg, 22 April 2022.

45 Senator R. Patrick, media release, 13 April 2022, www.rexpatrick.com.au/solomon_islands_intelligence_failure_underlines_the_need_for_parliamentary_scrutiny

46 A. Galloway and E. Bagshaw, 'Australian spy agency involved in Solomon Islands leak in last-ditch effort to stop deal', *SMH*, 23 April 2022.

47 National Security Archive, *US Intelligence and the Indian Bomb*, 13 April 2006, https://nsarchive2.gwu.edu/NSAEBB/NSAEBB187/index.htm

48 Aid/Watch, 'Submission to the Senate Inquiry into Australia's overseas aid and development assistance program', Australian Parliament House, 2014.

49 L. Eccles, 'Early Chinese accounts of Timor', in *Studies in Languages and Cultures of East Timor*, vol. 6, National Institute of Linguistics, Dili, 2004, p. 179.
50 R. Nakamura, 'US to build anti-China missile network along first island chain', *Nikkei Asia*, 5 March 2021.
51 C. Joye, 'Australia faces massive existential threat from China', *Australian Financial Review*, 24 April 2022.
52 N. Klein, 'Islands and rocks after the South China Sea arbitration', *Australian Year Book of International Law*, vol. 34, 2016.
53 Australian Antarctic Division, 'About Heard and McDonald Islands' (retrieved 20 April 2022), http://heardisland.antarctica.gov.au/about/human-activities.

5 EXPERTISE, SECRECY AND IDEOLOGY

1 Senate Foreign Affairs, Defence and Trade Legislation Committee, Estimates, 1 June 2021, pp. 28–9.
2 R. Ferguson, 'No military solution but "Taliban won't win"', *Australian*, 1 June 2021.
3 A. Dawi, 'US inspector questions top Ghani aide on corruption, collapse of Afghan government', Voice of America News, 1 February 2022.
4 A. Galloway, 'ADF chief says he was surprised by speed of Taliban takeover', *SMH*, 6 September 2021.
5 R. Devereaux, G. Greenwald and L. Poitras, 'The NSA is recording every cell phone call in the Bahamas', *Intercept*, 20 May 2014; A. Graef, 'Wikileaks reveals NSA is listening to nearly all calls in Afghanistan', UPI News, 23 May 2014, www.upi.com/Top_News/World-News/2014/05/23/

Wikileaks-reveals-NSA-is-listening-to-nearly-all-calls-in-Afghanistan/2781400880276

6 E. Groll, 'The United States has outspent the Marshall Plan to rebuild Afghanistan', *Foreign Policy*, 30 July 2014.

7 C. Helman and H. Tucker, 'The war in Afghanistan cost America $300 million per day for 20 years, with big bills yet to come', *Forbes*, 16 August 2021.

8 Senate Foreign Affairs, Defence and Trade References Committee, *Australia's Engagement in Afghanistan: Interim Report*, 2022, p. 226.

9 H. Kissinger, *American Foreign Policy*, W.W. Norton, New York, 1969, p. 28.

10 Joint Intelligence Committee (UK), 'International terrorism: War with Iraq', JIC Assessment, 10 February 2003 (retrieved 18 February 2022), http://webarchive.nationalarchives.gov.uk/20171123123130/http://www.iraqinquiry.org.uk/media/230918/2003-02-10-jic-assessment-international-terrorism-war-with-iraq.pdf

11 A. Palazzo, *The Australian Army and the War in Iraq, 2002–2010*, Directorate of Army Research and Analysis, Canberra, 2011, p. 37.

12 Ibid., p. 521.

13 Ibid., p. 521.

14 Ibid., p. 45.

15 L. Farrall, 'How al Qaeda works: What the organization's subsidiaries say about its strength', *Foreign Affairs*, vol. 90, no. 2, 2011, pp. 128–38.

16 A. Greene, 'Afghan soldier Hekmatullah, who killed three Australians, flown to Qatar ahead of peace talks with Taliban', ABC News, 11 September 2020.

17 G. Orwell, *The Complete Works of George Orwell*, ed. P. Davidson, vol. 8, Secker & Warburg, London, 1998, p. 100.

18 B. Bender, 'Taliban not main Afghan enemy: Few militants driven by religion, reports say', *Boston Globe*, 9 October 2009.

19 K. Foster, *Don't Mention the War*, Monash University Publishing, Clayton, 2013, p. 92.

20 L. Bartlett, interview with 6PR, 1 October 2021 (retrieved 18 February 2022), Australian Minister for Foreign Affairs and Minister for Women, www.foreignminister.gov.au

21 J. McGilvray, 'Common sense concepts: A Cartesian proposal', *Croatian Journal of Philosophy*, issue 9, 2003, pp. 275–88; M. Ledwig, *Common Sense: Its History, Method, and Applicability*, Peter Lang Publishing, New York, 2006; R. Descartes, *A Discourse on Method*, Part I, Clarendon Press, Oxford, 1937.

22 M. O'Connor, *An Act of War*, Arrow Australia, Sydney, 1990.

23 This is Bernard Keane's apt term.

24 S. Shrikhande, 'Australia–India: Alliances and self-reliance', Australian Naval Institute, 3 October 2021.

25 L. Brereton, 'Coming on top of India's three tests on Monday, this is an outrageous act of nuclear bastardry', news release, 21/98, 13 May 1998.

26 07CANBERRA1738_a, 'Meeting the Prime Minister', 10 December 2007, https://search.wikileaks.org/plusd/cables/07CANBERRA1738_a.html

27 N. Chomsky, *Deterring Democracy*, Hill & Wang, New York, 1992, p. 2.

28 R.J. McMahon, *The Cold War on the Periphery*, Columbia University Press, New York, 1994, pp. 62, 64, 89.
29 S.E. Graham and A. Davis, 'A "Hindu mystic" or a "Harrovian realist"? US, Australian and Canadian representations of Jawaharlal Nehru, 1947–1964', *Pacific Historical Review*, vol. 89, no. 2, 2020, pp. 198–231.
30 US Department of Defense, 'United States–Vietnam Relations, 1945–67', Draft revision of NSC 5429/5, 29 June 1959, US Government Printing Office, Washington, 1971, Book 10, pp. 1196–1210.
31 *Foreign Relations of the United States, 1955–1957*, vol. 8: South Asia, National Security Council Report, NSC 5701, 10 January 1957.
32 World Bank, *World Development Report*, World Bank, Washington DC, 1981, p. 85.
33 A. Tooze, 'China in 1983: A miracle waiting to happen?', *New Statesman*, 27 July 2021.
34 Global Hunger Index, 2021, p. 13, www.globalhungerindex.org
35 J. Drèze and A. Sen, *An Uncertain Glory: India and its Contradictions*, Princeton University Press, Princeton, 2013, pp. 73–4.
36 I. Weber, *How China Escaped Shock Therapy*, Routledge, London, 2021.
37 A.J. Nathan, 'The China threat in perspective', *Foreign Affairs*, vol. 101, issue 2, 2022, pp. 175–9.
38 White House, Memorandum for the President from Henry Kissinger, 'NSC Meeting, November 6—Chile', 5 November 1970, https://nsarchive.gwu.edu/document/20597-national-security-archive-doc-1-white-house

39 NSC, Memorandum of Conversation, NSC Meeting—Chile (NSSM 97), 6 November 1970. National Security Archive (gwu.edu).
40 Q. Slobodian, *Globalists: The End of Empire and the Birth of Neoliberalism*, Harvard University Press, Cambridge, 2018.
41 Senator A. Zakharov, *Senate Hansard*, 7 May 1985, p. 1423; Senator N. Bolkus, *Senate Hansard*, 11 September 1985, Canberra, p. 448.
42 S. Stern, *Battling for Hearts and Minds: Memory Struggles in Pinochet's Chile, 1973–1988*, Duke University Press, Durham, 2006, p. xxi.
43 T. Plibersek, 'National interest, good international citizenship and Labor's foreign policy', Lowy Institute, 31 May 2016.
44 Document 91, 21 February 1975, in W. Way (ed.), *Australia and the Indonesian Incorporation of Portuguese Timor, 1974–1976*, Melbourne University Press, Carlton, 2000.
45 Judgment 186, in *American Journal of International Law*, vol. 41, 1947, p. 172.
46 S. Staveteig, *How Many Persons in East Timor Went 'Missing' During the Indonesian Occupation? Results from Indirect Estimates*, International Institute for Applied Systems Analysis, Austria, 2007, p. 14; P. Job, *A Narrative of Denial: Australia and the Indonesian Violation of East Timor*, Melbourne University Press, Carlton, 2021.
47 H. Cohen, 'Did the walls have ears?', *Background Briefing*, ABC Radio National, 23 February 2014.
48 T. Stephens, 'Diplomat always at the centre: Ashton Calvert, 1945–2007', *SMH*, 23 November 2007.

49 A. Serdy, Supplementary Submission, Senate FADT Inquiry into Australia's declarations made under certain international laws, 2020.

50 Comissão de Acolhimento, Verdade e Reconciliac ão Timor Leste [Timor-Leste Commission for Reception, Truth and Reconciliation], *Final Report of the Commission*, vol. 3, Part 7.7: 'Rape, sexual slavery and other forms of sexual violence', Dili, Timor-Leste, 2006.

51 Job, *A Narrative of Denial*; C. Fernandes, 'Accomplice to mass atrocities', *Politics and Governance*, vol. 3, no. 4, 2015, pp. 1–11.

52 D. Lague, 'The looming crisis with Jakarta', *SMH*, 3 August 1996, p. 15.

53 C. Yarnell, 'Is the Australian public "rational" on foreign policy issues?', PhD thesis, University of Sydney, 2015, https://ses.library.usyd.edu.au/handle/2123/14427?show=full

54 B.C. Cohen, *The Press and Foreign Policy*, Princeton University Press, Princeton, 1963, p. 13.

55 R. Woolcott, cited in S. Burchill, 'East Timor, Australia, and Indonesia', *Bulletin of Concerned Asian Scholars*, vol. 32, nos 1 & 2, 2000, pp. 59–65.

56 Senator Lambie, Senate Hansard, 27 August 2014, pp. 5729–30.

57 Lowy Institute Poll, 2021, https://poll.lowyinstitute.org/themes/foreign-aid

6 NEITHER THEIR WAR NOR THEIR PEACE

1 For a case in point, see C. Fernandes, *Island off the Coast of Asia*, Monash University Publishing, Clayton, 2018, chapter 8.

2 P. Slezak, 'Let's keep the monarchy', *SMH*, 1 November 1999.

3 P. Hasluck, 'Australian foreign policy', *Current Notes on International Affairs*, vol. 38, no. 1, 1967.

4 T. Parsi, 'Why non-Western countries tend to see Russia's war very, very differently', Opinion, MSNBC, 12 April 2022, www.msnbc.com/opinion/msnbc-opinion/ukraine-russia-war-looks-very-different-outside-west-n1294280

5 A. de Zayas, *Building a Just World Order*, Clarity Press, Atlanta, 2021; UN General Assembly, 'Promotion of a democratic and equitable international order', A/RES/76/165, 16 December 2021.

6 S. Mettler and T. Brown, 'The growing rural–urban political divide and democratic vulnerability', *Annals of the American Academy of Political and Social Science*, vol. 699, no. 1, 2022, pp. 130–42.

Index